D1565010

THE COMPLETE HISTORY OF

RAILROADS

TRADE, TRANSPORT, AND EXPANSION

TRANSPORTATION AND SOCIETY

THE COMPLETE HISTORY OF

RAILROADS

TRADE, TRANSPORT, AND EXPANSION

EDITED BY ROBERT CURLEY, MANAGER, SCIENCE AND TECHNOLOGY

Britannica®
Educational Publishing

IN ASSOCIATION WITH

ROSEN
EDUCATIONAL SERVICES

Published in 2012 by Britannica Educational Publishing
(a trademark of Encyclopædia Britannica, Inc.)
in association with Rosen Educational Services, LLC
29 East 21st Street, New York, NY 10010.

First Edition

Britannica Educational Publishing
Michael I. Levy: Executive Editor
J.E. Luebering: Senior Manager
Adam Augustyn: Assistant Manager, Encyclopædia Britannica
Marilyn L. Barton: Senior Coordinator, Production Control
Steven Bosco: Director, Editorial Technologies
Lisa S. Braucher: Senior Producer and Data Editor
Yvette Charboneau: Senior Copy Editor
Kathy Nakamura: Manager, Media Acquisition
Robert Curley, Manager, Science and Technology

Rosen Educational Services
Nicholas Croce: Editor
Nelson Sá: Art Director
Cindy Reiman: Photography Manager
Karen Huang: Photo Researcher
Brian Garvey: Designer
Matt Cauli: Cover Design
Introduction by Joseph Kampff

Library of Congress Cataloging-in-Publication Data

The complete history of railroads: trade, transport, and expansion/edited by Robert
Curley.—1st ed.
    p. cm.—(Transportation and society)
"In association with Britannica Educational Publishing, Rosen Educational Services."
Includes bibliographical references and index.
ISBN 978-1-61530-681-7 (library binding)
1. Railroads—History. I. Curley, Robert, 1955–
TF15.C66 2012
385.09—dc23

                                                                      2011032959

Manufactured in the United States of America

On the cover: A high-speed commuter train. *Shutterstock.com*

On page xii-xiii: Front locomotive of Conrail train. *Marty Katz/Time & Life Pictures/Getty Images*

On pages 1, 18, 48, 71, 88, 108, 134, 164, 176, 204, 223, 226, 229: The passenger car of a locomotive. *Shutterstock.com*

CONTENTS

52

62

90

109

110

129

136

146

165

INTRODUCTION

The global village in which many 21st-century people live depends on extensive and efficient networks. Technological networks have made the world smaller and more accessible at the same time as they have made it larger by helping to increase the knowledge we have of the world. The modes of transportation and the networks that support them today, which carry people and objects over vast expanses with a swiftness that is unprecedented in human history, are just as vital to today's world as the communication networks that allow people to transmit information across the globe in the blink of an eye. Yet, although this efficiency is a relatively new phenomenon, the speed with which human beings are able to travel throughout the world, transport objects, and exchange information is often taken for granted today. It is important, therefore, constantly to ask the questions: How did we get to where we are today? What brought us to this point? By tracking the history of the railroads—one of the world's most important and innovative technological networks—from the rudimentary plateways that supported wooden carts in the 16th century to the high-speed passenger lines of today, *The Complete History of Railroads* shows the crucial role railroads have played in bringing human beings into the modern world.

The provenance of today's railroads can be discovered in Europe during the Middle Ages in the plateways that were developed to facilitate overland transport of cargo where canals and other waterways were unavailable. These plateways—which tended to consist of two parallel strips of pavement—provided a smooth and stable surface for wagons to ride on that allowed the wagons to convey heavier loads with greater speeds over long distances. Although they may not be immediately recognizable as such for many people today, the plateways of the Middle Ages represent the world's first railroads. And even in this unrefined form, the first railroads' purpose was remarkably similar to that of the railroads today: to use the most advanced technology available in order to extend the range and increase the efficiency of the world's transportation networks. By the opening of the 18th century, extensive networks of plateways were already well in place in many of the important mining centres of Europe. Nevertheless, it was not until the development of the steam engine for use on the railroads in the 19th century that railroads truly began to resemble what they are today.

Railroad technology, stimulated by and urging on the Industrial Revolution, improved considerably in the 19th century as sophisticated railroad systems were developed concurrently in Britain and the United States. In Britain, the railroads' value as a practical and adaptable mode of transportation for cargo as well as for people was established in 1830 with the opening of the Liverpool and Manchester Railway. This railroad operated with an all-steam powered locomotive, the *Rocket*. This early steam-powered locomotive, engineered by George Stephenson and his son, Robert, was capable of travelling at the then impressive speed of 36 miles (58 km) per hour. By 1889, advances in railroad technology in Europe would allow people to travel over 1,700 miles (about 2,740 km) of continuous rail between Paris and Constantinople in the luxurious comfort of Georges Nagelmacker's Orient-Express, Europe's first transcontinental railroad.

While engineers in the United States created sophisticated railroad systems at approximately the same time as they arose in Britain, the demands of the largely undeveloped American landscape, coupled with America's less than optimal economic situation, required the American railroad's development to follow a decidedly different track than it did in Britain. British railroad technologies simply did not hold up well in America. To make travel over America's steeper grades possible, the United States needed its locomotives to be more powerful than their British counterparts. At the same time, America needed more dependable, durable, and less expensive rails than those used in Britain. Innovative American engineers, such as those in Baltimore, Maryland, along with the shrewd financiers of the American Northeast—particularly in Boston, Massachusetts—were able to meet the technological and financial demands of America's burgeoning railroads. By the 1850s, railroads linked many of the most important eastern American cities, and America's own transcontinental railroad was just around the bend. American railroad systems continued to improve and expand throughout the 19th century. By 1910, long before the construction of America's interstate highways, extensive networks of rails linked up diverse regions of the United States and Canada, and the reputation of the American railroad was solidly established.

In order to meet the demands of a constantly changing world for increased speed and efficiency, locomotive technology continued to develop over the course of the railroad's history. Steam-powered locomotives—operating on principles first demonstrated in Stephenson's original *Rocket*—proved suited to the task for quite some time, remaining in widespread use until around the end of World War II. What is perhaps one of the world's most recognizable steam locomotives, the *Big Boy*, was also one of the world's largest and most powerful. The Union Pacific Railroad's *Big Boys* were manufactured between 1941 and 1944 to carry cargo over the steep grades presented by the mountainous terrain of the Western United States. These giants of the rails—they weighed 604 tons and spanned over 40 meters (132 feet)—were able to attain a top speed of 70 miles (712 km) per hour while pulling a loaded train. Although the *Big Boys* and other steam locomotives were phased out of use, eventually giving way to more efficient diesel and electric locomotives in the second half of the 20th century, steam-powered locomotives remain a symbol of speed and sheer power in the public imagination today.

In the United States, the always audible call for increased speed and greater economic efficiency dictated the replacement of all steam locomotives with diesel-powered locomotives by the end of the 1960s. Because they can operate for over 2,000 miles (over 3,200 km) without stopping for maintenance, diesel traction systems proved far more economical than the outmoded, high-maintenance steam-powered locomotives they replaced. Diesel locomotives use fuel much more efficiently than steam-powered locomotives and at the time offer the additional advantages of faster, smoother acceleration and higher top speeds. Diesel-electric trains combine the benefits of diesel and electric propulsion while reducing the high initial costs of an all-electric line by using diesel fuel to generate electricity within the locomotive. The more fuel-efficient diesel-electric system is suitable for many freight and passenger lines, but because diesel-electric locomotives can only generate the horsepower of their diesel engines, they are unable to achieve the high speeds produced by all-electric traction systems.

Although one of the earliest commercial electrified railroads was developed in the United States, electrified lines did not catch on as well in America as they did in other parts of the world. Electrified railroads achieved particular success in Europe. In Switzerland, for example, 96.6 percent of the national rail system's length operates with electric traction. And Belgium, Sweden, Austria, and Italy employ around 60 percent electric traction for their national rail systems, compared to less than 1 percent in the United States. Although there are some disadvantages to electric traction systems—the high costs of maintaining the central power plant, for example—electricity is widely held to be the most efficient and economic source of locomotive power. Electric locomotives are prevalent in today's metropolitan rail systems and high-speed passenger rails, such as the Shinkansen lines of Japan.

The Shinkansen high-speed rail system opened in 1964, with the original line linking the important metropolitan and industrial centers of Tokyo and Osaka. Known as "the bullet train," the first trains on the system were capable of reaching top speeds of 130 miles (210 km) per hour. Today, the Shinkansen network reaches many cities on the islands of Honshu and Kyushu, and because of technological innovation, passenger trains are able to attain top velocities of up to 185 miles (300 km) per hour—a far cry from Stephenson's 36-mile (58-km)-per-hour steam-powered *Rocket*. Because of the greatly increased speeds and considerable complexity of today's railroad networks, efficient communication methods are crucial. A centralized traffic control facility in Tokyo precisely oversees every Shinkansen train's operation using advanced computer technology.

Throughout their history, railroad systems have employed the most advanced communications technologies available to ensure the speed, safety, and efficiency of their trains. For example, railroad companies were the first to use the electric telegraph and telephone in their day-to-day operations. The railroads also explored the new communications possibilities presented by radio technology early in its development. After the introduction of sophisticated two-way radios by the close of World War II, the railroad industry was effectively able to use radio on a large scale, streamlining track maintenance and facilitating the smooth functioning of switching yards. Eventually, microwave radio replaced the cumbersome telegraph lines that often ran parallel with the railroad tracks. In addition, many railroads today are using versatile, optical-fibre technology to transmit video, data, and speech throughout their networks with an immediacy that was unimaginable until recently.

Computers have made everything faster and better organized in today's societies, and railroads quickly adopted computer technology to help them further meet their requirements for speed and productivity. Integrated computer systems provide quick and accurate data on nearly every aspect of railroad operations, dramatically increasing the railroad's already remarkable capacity to meet the transport demands of the modern world. From the design, manufacture, and maintenance of train and locomotive components, to the creation of and adherence to timetables through the precise controlling of the spacing of trains, to the ready availability of online ticketing and trip planning, computers have become an indispensable element of railroad systems today.

By tracing the history of the railroads, it is possible to bridge the gap in the popular imagination between the Middle Ages and the post-industrial Information Age that we inhabit today. It comes as no surprise, then, that the rapid development and expansion of rail transportation during the Industrial Revolution prompted advances in bridge design as new bridges were constructed to accommodate the weight of the locomotives. With the construction of his bridge designs, Robert Stephenson reinforced his status as one of the world's great innovative engineers. Stephenson's Britannia Bridge in northern Wales—completed in 1850 and still in use today—was one of the first bridges built specifically for use by the railroad.

Gustav Eiffel, another familiar figure, was also an important builder of early railroad bridges. One can easily detect the beginnings of the Eiffel Tower in Eiffel's innovative use of wrought-iron towers in the viaducts he constructed for the railways in France between 1867 and 1869. Gustav Eiffel's Garabit Viaduct spanned the Truyère River, which at a length of 162 metres (541 feet) was the longest viaduct in the world when it opened in 1884. Thus, we can see that the railroad has consistently inspired technological innovation throughout its history.

Since their beginnings in support of the canal networks of the Middle Ages, the railroads have enjoyed a rich and varied history. And even though the railroads have changed significantly over time, their chief aims have remained the same: To use the newest technologies to increase the speed, efficiency, and the range of their networks. Today, railroads continue to advance on the cutting edge of technology as they move into the future, producing trains that are faster and more efficient for passengers and freight. While older lines are continually updated and maintained, new tracks are constantly being set down. The railroads continue to stretch their network of rails into newly developing parts of the world, expanding the global village. When we ask ourselves in the 21st century: What brought us to this point? How did we get here? It is possible to answer without hesitation: We came by rail.

CHAPTER 1

THE FIRST RAILROADS

The earliest railroads reinforced transportation patterns that had developed centuries before. During the Middle Ages most heavy or bulky items were carried by water wherever possible. Where natural interconnection among navigable rivers was lacking, gaps in trade were likely to develop, most notably at watersheds. By the 16th century canal building was being widely used in Europe to integrate waterway systems based on natural streams. During the Industrial Revolution canal networks became urgent necessities in western Europe and the western Mediterranean. In Britain and France the increased use of coal for raising steam and for iron smelting greatly increased the need for canal transportation. In the 50 years after 1775 England and Wales were webbed with canals to provide reasonably inexpensive transport of coal. But in areas of concentrated industry in hilly country, such as around Birmingham and in the "Black Country" of England, or areas of heavy coal production in droughty uplands, as in western County Durham, the transporting of coal by water seemed impracticable.

EARLY EUROPEAN RAILROADS

A development of the late Middle Ages, the plateway suggested a means to make steam-powered land transport practicable. In central Europe most of the common metals were being mined by the 16th and 17th centuries, but, because they occurred in low concentrations, great tonnages of ore had to be mined to produce small yields of usable material. In that situation it was helpful to provide a supporting pavement on which wheels might run with somewhat reduced friction. Recourse was had to the minimum pavement possible, that provided by two parallel rails or plates supporting the wheels of a wagon. The wheels were guided by a flange either on the rail or on the wheel. The latter was ultimately preferred, because with the flange on the wheel debris was less likely to lodge on the rail. In the Harz Mountains, the Black Forest, the Ore Mountains, the Vosges, Steiermark, and other mining areas such railroads or plateways were widespread before the 18th century.

The bulk and weight of the steam engine suggested its being mounted on a railway. This occurred in Britain where, in the 17th century, coal mining had become common in the northeast in Tyneside and in South Wales. By 1800 each of these areas also had an extensive plateway system depending on gravity-induced movement or animal traction. The substitution of steam-engine traction was logical. The timing of this shift during the first decade of the 19th century was dictated by improvements in the steam engine. The weight-to-power ratio was unfavourable until 1804, when a Cornish engineer, Richard Trevithick, constructed a steam engine of his own design. In 1802 at Coalbrookdale in Shropshire he built a steam-pumping engine that operated at 145 pounds per square inch pressure (roughly 1,000 kilopascals). He mounted the high-pressure engine on a car with wheels set to operate on the rails of a cast-iron tramroad located at Pen-y-Darren, Wales.

THE STOCKTON AND DARLINGTON RAILWAY

George Stephenson was the son of a mechanic and, because of his skill at operating Newcomen engines, served as chief mechanic at the Killingworth colliery northwest of Newcastle upon Tyne, Eng. In 1813 he examined the first practical and successful steam locomotive, that of John Blenkinsop, and, convinced that he could offer improvements, designed and built the *Blücher* in 1814. Later he introduced the "steam blast," by which exhaust was directed up the chimney, pulling air after it and increasing the draft. His success in designing several more locomotives brought him to the attention of the planners of a proposed railway linking the port of Stockton with Darlington, 8 miles (13 km) inland.

Investment in the Bishop Auckland coalfield of western County Durham was heavily concentrated in Darlington, where there was agitation for improvement in the outward shipment of the increasing tonnages produced. The region had become the most extensive producer of coal, most of which was sent by coastal sloop to the London market. The

The opening of the Stockton and Darlington Railway on September 27, 1825.
Rischgitz/Hulton Archive/Getty Images

mining moved inland toward the Pennine ridge and thus farther from the port at Stockton-on-Tees, which in 1810 had been made a true seaport by completion of the Tees Navigation. A canal linking the cities had been proposed in a survey by James Brindley as early as 1769 but was rejected because of cost, and by the early 19th century several of the gravity tramways or railways on Tyneside had been fitted with primitive locomotives. In 1818 the promoters settled on the construction of a railway, and in April 1821 parliamentary authorization was gained and George IV gave his assent.

While construction was under way on the 25-mile (40-km) single-track line it was decided to use locomotive engines as well as horse traction. Construction began on May 13, 1822, using both malleable iron rails (for two-thirds the distance) and cast iron and set at a track gauge of 4 feet 8 inches (1,422 mm). This gauge was subsequently standardized, with one-half inch added at a date and for reasons unknown.

On Sept. 27, 1825, the Stockton and Darlington Railway was completed and opened for common carrier service between docks at Stockton and the Witton Park colliery in the western part of the county of Durham. It was authorized to carry both passengers and freight. From the beginning it was the first railroad to operate as a common carrier open to all shippers. Coal brought to Stockton for sale in the coastal trade dropped in price from 18 shillings to 12 shillings a ton. At that price the demand for coal was greater than the initial fabric of the Stockton and Darlington could handle.

This was an experimental line. Passenger service, offered by contractors who placed coach bodies on flat-cars, did not become permanent until 1833, and horse traction was commonly used for passenger haulage at first. But after two years' operation the trade between Stockton and Darlington had grown tenfold.

THE LIVERPOOL AND MANCHESTER RAILWAY

The Liverpool and Manchester, Stephenson's second project, can logically be thought of as the first fully evolved railway to be built. It was intended to provide an extensive passenger service and to rely on locomotive traction alone. The Rainhill locomotive trials were conducted in 1829 to assure that those prime movers would be adequate to the demands placed on them and that adhesion was practicable. Stephenson's entry, the *Rocket*, won the trials owing to the increased power provided by its multiple fire-tube boiler. The rail line began in a long tunnel from the docks in Liverpool, and the Edgehill Cutting through which it passed dropped the line to a lower elevation across the low plateau above the city. Embankments were raised above the level of the Lancashire Plain to improve the drainage of the line and to reduce grades on a gently rolling natural surface. A firm causeway was pushed across Chat Moss (swamp) to complete the line's quite considerable engineering works.

When the 30-mile (50-km) line was opened to traffic in 1830 the utility of railroads received their ultimate test. Though its cost had been more than £40,000 per mile and it could no longer be held that the railroad was a cheaper form of transportation than the canal, the Liverpool and Manchester demonstrated the railways' adaptability to diverse transportation needs and volumes.

CHARACTERISTICS OF BRITISH RAILROADS

Not all British railways were so heavily engineered as the Liverpool and Manchester line, but in general terms they were normally constructed to a high standard. Most main

lines were double-tracked, were carried on a grade separated from the road network, and were built to make the
job of locomotive traction easier. Stephenson believed
that grades should be less than 1 percent—substantially
less if at all possible—and that curves should have very
wide radii, perhaps half a mile or more. Because capital was
used somewhat lavishly in right-of-way construction and
infrastructure, it was the practice to employ locomotives
stingily. Power was used economically, and wheels came
off the tracks easily. When a line, such as the Worcester
and Birmingham Railway, had to be built on a steep grade
(2.68 percent), it proved necessary to purchase American
locomotives for successful adhesion.

THE ROCKET

Following the success of the Stockton and Darlington Railway in 1825,
the cities of Liverpool and Manchester decided to build a 40-mile
(64-km) steam-operated line connecting them. George Stephenson
was entrusted with constructing the line, but to choose a locomotive a competition was held. Stephenson joined forces with his son,
Robert, and together the Stephensons built a pioneering locomotive,
the *Rocket*, that won against three rivals—including an entry by John
Ericsson, a Swedish-born engineer who later designed an ironclad
vessel called the *Monitor* for the U.S. Navy during the American Civil
War. For a short stretch the *Rocket* achieved a speed of 36 miles (58
km) per hour. It was much modified during its subsequent service life,
and today it is on display at the Science Museum, London.

The principles established by the Stephensons with the *Rocket*
remained essentially the same for the rest of the steam era: horizontal
cylinders mounted beneath a multitubular boiler with a firebox at the
rear and a tender carrying supplies of water and fuel. The Liverpool
and Manchester Railway was the first fully timetabled railway service with scheduled freight and passenger traffic relying entirely on
the steam locomotive for traction. Its opening in 1830 may fairly be
regarded as the inauguration of the railway era.

The national pattern of rails in Britain radiated from London. The early London and Birmingham became ultimately the London, Midland, and Scottish; the London and York line became the Great Northern Railway; the Great Western expanded into a network of most of the western lines; and the Southern Railway provided lines for several boat and ferry trains. All companies ultimately wove dense webs of commuter lines around London, Manchester, Birmingham, Glasgow, Cardiff, and Edinburgh. Ultimately there was competition between companies, particularly on the longer runs such as those to Scotland, Wales, and the southwest.

Because there were limited regional monopolies, in the beginning railway companies established individual terminal stations in London and individual through stations in the provincial cities reached by their monopoly line. By the second half of the 19th century this situation led to a need for interstation local transportation in London, Liverpool, and Glasgow.

THE RAILROAD IN CONTINENTAL EUROPE

Development of the railroad in France was somewhat independent of that in Britain. Differences included the use of high-pressure steam multitube boilers (for quick recovery of steam after a pressing demand) and variations in locomotive design. There were certain consistencies, however. It was the transport of coal that frequently determined whether railroads were constructed and where they would run. The earliest rail line in France was in the Stéphanoise coalfield southwest of Lyon. Later, in the Grand-Hornu colliery at St. Ghislain, the first Belgian railroad was constructed.

In Europe the railroad became an instrument of geopolitics early on. The "Belgian Revolution" of 1830 (against

Dutch control within a joint monarchy), which had notable British support, left the newly established kingdom rather blocked as to transportation because the medieval waterway system on the Meuse and the Schelde flowed to the sea through the Netherlands. When the Dutch blockaded port traffic, the Belgians were forced to turn to a system of railways constructed according to plans and technologies supplied by George Stephenson. New ports were built on the Channel coast, and the world's first international rail line ran between Liège and Cologne. By building an extensive system of rail lines Prussia ultimately forced a unification of the German states under its own leadership. In similar fashion the Kingdom of Piedmont, through its rail lines, brought pressure on the Italian states to join in a united country about 1860.

Although British railways were privately built, it was far more common on the Continent that rail construction was undertaken directly by the state. Such was the case in Belgium, where the national treasury paid for the interchange of main railroads (from Ostend to the German border and from the Netherlands to France) that met at Mechelen. The earliest French coal-carrying lines were privately built, but a national system was established in 1842. Six large companies were granted charters to operate, five in vectors from Paris (Nord, Est, Paris-Lyon-Marseille [originally only as far as Dijon], Orléans, West, the "State" line to Le Havre, and the Compagnie du Midi between Bordeaux and Marseille). Under this plan the infrastructure was designed and executed under the supervision of the Corps de Ponts et Chaussées and paid for by the state. The superstructure of ballast, tracks, signals, rolling stock, stations, and operating capital came from the private companies. These charters were normally granted for more than 100 years, but they were abolished in 1938 when the Société Nationale des Chemins de Fer Française

A French National Railways ticket hall at the Gare d'Austerlitz in Paris, circa 1972. Keystone/Hulton Archive/Getty Images

(SNCF; French National Railways) was formed. By 1945 almost all main rail lines in Europe were nationalized, except for significant exceptions in the remaining narrow-gauge lines of Switzerland and France.

Construction of railroads in the German states came at an earlier stage of economic development than was the case in England, Belgium, or France. The first rail lines in most of western Europe were in existence by 1835, but at that time Germany was still quite rural in settlement and development patterns. There had been little accumulation of industrial capital, the backbone of much rail investment elsewhere.

A final aspect of European rail construction is found in what might be called the "defensive use of gauge." When the first Russian lines were built there was no effort made to adapt the English standard gauge of 4 feet 8.5 inches (1,435 mm), despite the fact that it was common throughout western Europe (save in Ireland, Spain, and Portugal) as well as in much of the United States and Canada. It was the deliberate policy of Spain, and thereby of Portugal, to adopt a nominal gauge of 5 feet 6 inches (1,676 mm), so as to be distinct from France, a neighbour who on several occasions during the preceding century had interfered in Spanish affairs. In the Russian case it seems not to have been so much a policy of military defense as it was of the tsar having chosen an American engineer to plan his railroads in an era when gauges were not truly standardized in the United States. The 5-foot (1,524-mm) gauge that Major George Whistler of the Baltimore and Ohio Railroad proposed for Russia was the same as the regional "Southern" gauge adopted by John Jervis for the South Carolina Railroad in 1833.

EARLY AMERICAN RAILROADS

As in England, the adoption of a railed pavement in North America was originally tied to gravity operation but later was adapted for the locomotive. In the United States the earliest railed pavements were in or adjacent to Boston, where in 1807 (when it was decided to flatten the top of Beacon Hill in order to enlarge the Massachusetts statehouse) a tramway was constructed to carry gravel to the base of the hill to begin filling the Back Bay. The first railway in Canada was constructed by British military engineers in the 1820s at the Citadel at Québec city; it used a similar cable-operated tramway to ascend the heights of Cape Diamond. But it was in 1825 on the Granite Railroad just south of Boston on the side of Great Blue Hill that

THE ORIENT EXPRESS

The *Orient-Express* was a luxury train that ran from Paris to Constantinople (Istanbul) for more than 80 years (1883–1977). Europe's first transcontinental express, it initially covered a route of about 1,700 miles (2,700 km) that included brief stopovers in such cities as Munich, Vienna, Budapest, and Bucharest. Its service was stopped by World War I but resumed in 1919, with the route running from Calais and Paris to Lausanne, then via the Simplon Pass to Milan, Venice, Zagreb, Belgrade, and Sofia; the train was then called the *Simplon–Orient-Express*. Interrupted again during World War II, service resumed in 1947.

The *Orient-Express* was developed by the Belgian businessman Georges Nagelmackers and made its inaugural run in 1883. During its first journey the passengers travelled from Paris to the Bulgarian port of Varna via train and were then ferried by steamship across the Black Sea to Constantinople. By 1889, however, the entire trip was by rail. Nagelmackers' firm, La Compagnie Internationale des Wagons-Lits et des Grands Express Européens, furnished the train, which had sleeping, restaurant, and salon cars that housed smoking compartments and ladies' drawing rooms. With its Oriental rugs, velvet draperies, mahogany paneling, deep armchairs covered in soft Spanish leather, and fine cuisine, the *Orient-Express* was unmatched in luxuriousness and comfort. For years it attracted the elite of Europe's society, including royalty. The glamour of the train also caught the imagination of numerous writers, among them Graham Greene and Agatha Christie, whose works *Stamboul Train* (1932) and *Murder on the Orient Express* (1933) helped to make it world-famous.

The *Orient-Express* was discontinued in 1977 after several decades of steadily declining ridership. In 1982, an American, James Sherwood, revived the train as the *Venice Simplon–Orient-Express*, with several routes between London and Venice—and, subsequently, several other routes through central and eastern Europe, including Paris-Istanbul.

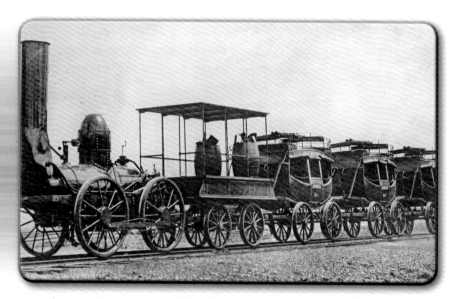

The steam locomotive De Witt Clinton (1831), built for the Mohawk and Hudson Railroad, New York state. Encyclopædia Britannica, Inc.

several of the characteristic features of American railroading, such as the swiveling truck and the four-wheel truck, were first put into use.

In 1805 Oliver Evans, a Delaware wheelwright, built an engine with steam pressure well above the single atmosphere that Scottish engineer James Watt had used in his early engines. Evans was commissioned to construct a steam-powered dredge to be used on the docks in Philadelphia. He built his dredge away from the Schuylkill River, having it move itself, ponderously, to its destination by rail. Nevertheless, the earliest locomotives used in North America were of British design. In 1829 the *Stourbridge Lion* was the first to run on a North American railroad. But on the Delaware and Hudson Railroad, where the *Stourbridge Lion* ran, as on the Champlain and St. Lawrence Railroad, the first in Canada, Stephenson locomotives proved unsuited to the crude track and quickly derailed. The British locomotive had virtually no constructive impact on North American locomotives. The only residual characteristic was the 4-foot, 8.5-inch (1,435-mm) gauge, which was often thought to be a misfortune in being too narrow.

It was the brute strength of American locomotives, their great tolerance of cheap and crude track, their durability, their economy of operation, and their simplicity of maintenance that determined almost from the first years of operation that there would be a distinctively American railroad sharing little with British practice. It seems reasonable to argue that once the British had shown that railroads could be made to work the Americans reinvented them for a very different terrain, economic climate, and demographic level. The creation of the American railroad was a contemporaneous but not a derivative development.

The American railroad came into existence because incomplete geographic knowledge caused the first British colonists to plant early entrepôts in what were later understood to be unfavourable locations. The uplands in central Massachusetts were already being abandoned for agricultural use when the railroad arrived in that region in the mid-1830s. Only when in the 1840s a railroad reached into the

Matthew Boulton and James Watt; painting on tile by John Eyre, 1886. SSPL via Getty Images

agricultural belt in the American Midwest could the port of Boston find a truly great hinterland. And by 1825 the Erie Canal had created a water connection between the Midwest and the port of New York.

Two other colonial ports mirrored the conditions in Boston. In Maryland, the rivers did not serve the colonial port at Baltimore. The Susquehanna just to the north and the Potomac just to the south had falls near their mouths. A port had grown up at Alexandria on the Virginia side of the Potomac; and the Commonwealth of Pennsylvania built a canal and later a railroad to keep inland trade from passing southward to Baltimore. In South Carolina the main port, Charleston, was, like Boston, on a short stream offering little access to the interior.

These "mislocated" colonial ports were among the largest American cities, but they were denied the easy access to the interior that seemed essential for growth as the country spread inward. The creation of the railroad offered a solution to the access problem. Competition among the Atlantic ports meant that those with the poorest river connections to the West—Baltimore, Boston, and Charleston—became the earliest and strongest proponents of railroad promotion.

THE BALTIMORE AND OHIO RAILROAD

The first to take an active role was Baltimore, which in the 1820s had become the second largest American city. On July 4, 1828, Baltimore merchants began the construction of a railroad from the harbour to some point, then undetermined, on the Ohio River. The results of adopting British practice were generally bad, forcing the engineers to design a railroad from scratch. Locomotives designed and built in Baltimore were stronger than those of Robert

Stephenson. Leveling rods kept those locomotives on the relatively poor track, and a swiveling leading truck guided them into tight curves. On the Camden and Amboy Railroad, another pioneering line, the engineer John Jervis invented the T-cross-section rail that greatly cheapened and simplified the laying of track when combined with the wooden crosstie also first introduced in the United States. Simplicity and strength became the basic test for railroad components in North America. On cars the individual trucks were given four wheels to allow heavier loads to be carried, and the outside dimensions of cars were enlarged.

In western Maryland the engineers were faced with their steepest grades. These came to be known as the "ruling grade"—that is, the amount of locomotive power required for the transit of a line was determined by its steepest grade. Robert Stephenson had thought 1 percent was the steepest grade a locomotive could surmount. At the top of the climb over the Allegheny Front the Baltimore and Ohio (B&O) engineers had to accept a 17-mile (27-km) grade of about 2.2 percent, which they managed to achieve with the stronger American engines. Adopted later as the ruling grade for the Canadian Pacific and a number of other North American lines, the 2.2 percent figure has become so fixed that it now ranks second only to standard gauge as a characteristic of the North American railroad.

The B&O was finally completed in December 1852 to Wheeling, Va. (now West Virginia). But by that time it was only the first of what turned out to be six trans-Appalachian railroads completed in 1851–52.

BOSTON RAILROADS

Three Massachusetts railroads were chartered and under construction in 1830, at first showing a strong affinity for British practice. The Boston and Lowell, Boston and Providence, and Boston and Worcester railroads radiated from the metropolis to towns no more than 45 miles (70 km) away. In 1835, when all were operating, Boston became the world's first rail hub. As in Europe the pattern of having a metropolitan station for each line was established, though Boston had by the end of the century created a North Union Station and a South Station and an elevated railway to join them by rapid transit. Boston's main contribution to the development of railroads was made in finance rather than in technology. The merchants who were interested in extending the city's trade inland had invested actively in the 1830s, and by the 1840s they had connected all of New England to their port; but extending their influence farther was severely constrained by New York state. The New York legislature was unsympathetic to chartering a rail line projected from Boston. Boston capital's role in American railroading came through investment in distant and detached railroads. It first gained control of the Michigan Central Railroad, then of its physical extension, the Chicago, Burlington, and Quincy Railroad. This capital trail continued as Boston money dominated the Union Pacific; the Atchison, Topeka & Santa Fe Railway; and other important western lines.

THE SOUTH CAROLINA RAILROAD

Merchants in Charleston launched an early railroad—the South Carolina Railroad—which at 130 miles (209 km) was by some measure the longest rail line in the world when it opened in 1833. But it was constructed very cheaply. Where it could not be laid on crossties placed directly on the flat or gently sloping surface of the Atlantic Coastal Plain, it was borne on short posts that were intended to permit surface wash to pass beneath the track. Much of this fabric later had to be improved. The object of the Charlestonians was to divert the flow of cotton from the port of Savannah, Ga., to the older and larger South Carolina port. Theirs was considered mainly as a regional rail line, which began service with a single locomotive. The hope was that the early years of operation would earn enough profit that the line might be improved on retained earnings and that success for the sponsoring port would come from increased trade at its docks and from the extension of the line to tap a wider hinterland.

CHAPTER 2

The Development of Modern Railroads

Through the 19th and 20th centuries, railroads spread over the European and North American continents and made their presence in the rest of the world as well. For a century or more they were the dominant land transportation, moving raw materials, goods, and people at a speed never before dreamed possible. Steam propulsion was brought to its greatest power and efficiency, then made way for electricity and diesel power. Even as these technologies developed, however, other modes of transport, particularly the airplane and automobile, rose to prominence, at least in the movement of people. Railroads no longer dominate surface transportation, though they are still very important and are still undergoing technical improvement.

AMERICAN RAILROADS

The first phase of American railroad development, from 1828 until about 1850, most commonly involved connecting two relatively large cities that were fairly close neighbours. New York City and New Haven, Conn., Richmond, Va., and Washington, D.C., or Syracuse, N.Y., and Rochester, N.Y., were examples of this phase of eastern railroad development. By 1852 this first phase was followed by six crossings of the Appalachian mountain chain, which were essentially incremental alignments of railroads first proposed to tie neighbouring cities together, and there was a

A train crossing a bridge on the Baltimore to Ohio railroad in 1858. Hulton Archive/Getty Images

need for a new strategy of routing. What followed was an extension of railroads into the interior of the continent and from the Atlantic to the Pacific.

EXPANSION INTO THE INTERIOR

In the 1850s and '60s the B&O projected a line from Wheeling to Cincinnati, Ohio, and from Cincinnati to the east bank of the Mississippi opposite St. Louis, then the greatest mercantile city in the American interior. The Pennsylvania Railroad reached Pittsburgh in 1852; and the company began to seek the merger of second-phase railroads in the Midwest into a line from Pittsburgh to Ft. Wayne, Ind., and thence to Chicago, which was emerging as the dominant junction of the vastly productive agricultural and industrial region of the eastern prairie states. The first railroad from the east reached Chicago in February

1852, and soon thereafter lines were pushed onward toward the Mississippi and the Missouri rivers. In 1859 the Hannibal and St. Joseph Railroad was completed to the middle Missouri valley; it remained the most westerly thrust of railroad during the Civil War. By the beginning of the 1850s it had already become clear that there would be considerable pressure to undertake a transcontinental railroad.

THE TRANSCONTINENTAL RAILROAD

The first public proposal for such a line was made by the New York City merchant Asa Whitney in 1844. At that time the United States did not hold outright possession of land west of the Rockies, though it exercised joint

The building of the Transcontinental Railroad, circa 1869. Fotosearch/ Archive Photo/Getty Images

occupation of the Oregon Country until 1846, when under a treaty with Britain it gained possession of the Pacific coast between the 42nd and 49th parallels. Whitney's Railroad Convention proposed a line from the head of the Great Lakes at Duluth, Minn., to the Oregon Country. The Mexican War, by adding California, Arizona, and New Mexico to the American domain, complicated the matter greatly. North-South sectionalism intruded when it was appreciated that west of the Missouri any rail project would require a combination of federal and private efforts, the American practice. In the hope of resolving the regional conflict, the Corps of Topographic Engineers was authorized in 1854 to undertake the Pacific Railroad Survey, which studied almost all the potential rail routes in the West.

The survey on the 49th parallel was in the mid-1890s transformed into the Great Northern Railway. A near neighbour, the 47th parallel survey, had in the early 1880s been followed by the Northern Pacific Railway. The 41st parallel survey, only a partial investigation, sketched the alignment on which was to be built the first transcontinental railroad, the Union Pacific east of Great Salt Lake and the Central Pacific west thereof. The 35th parallel route became the Rock Island line from Memphis to Tucumcari, N.M., and westward from there the Atchison, Topeka, and Santa Fe Railway to Los Angeles. The southernmost route, the 32nd parallel, was to run from Shreveport, La., across Texas and then, through the Gadsden Purchase of 1853, to San Diego; this route became the Southern Pacific line from Los Angeles to El Paso.

Construction began in 1862 of the 41st parallel route, which had been selected to receive federal grants, but because of the outbreak of the Civil War relatively little was accomplished on the Union Pacific Railroad before the end of fighting in 1865. In California, little affected

THE PACIFIC RAILWAY ACTS

The Pacific Railway Acts were two measures that provided federal subsidies in land and loans for the construction of a transcontinental railroad across the United States.

The first Pacific Railway Act (July 1, 1862) authorized the building of the railroad and granted rights of way to the Union Pacific to build westward from Omaha, Neb., and to the Central Pacific to build eastward from Sacramento, Calif. The act also granted 10 alternate sections of public domain land per mile on both sides of the railway, and it provided loan bonds for each mile of track laid. The loans were repayable in 30 years, and the dollars per mile escalated in accord with the difficulty of the terrain.

Two years later, the railroads were still hampered in their quest for sufficient capital for the vast construction project. Congress obliged with the second Pacific Railway Act (July 2, 1864), which doubled the size of the land grants and allowed the railroads to sell their own bonds. After the transcontinental railroad was completed in 1869, congressional investigations revealed that some railroad entrepreneurs had illegally profiteered from the two Pacific Railway Acts.

by the war, construction was more rapidly advanced. By 1865 the original juncture of the Central Pacific and Union Pacific was moved eastward; the meeting took place on May 10, 1869, at Promontory, Utah.

The opening of the Pacific railroad in 1869 demonstrated that the market for the profitable operation of such a line still lay somewhat in the future: one eastbound and one westbound train a week were adequate to meet the demands of traffic. It took almost a generation before additional rail lines to the West Coast seemed justified. In 1885 the Santa Fe reached the Los Angeles basin and the Northern Pacific Railway reached Puget Sound. Each western railroad now had to shape a new economic and geographic strategy. In place of the natural territory gained through monopoly the western lines tried to accomplish regional ubiquity, under which the Southern Pacific (originally the Central Pacific), the Union Pacific, or the Santa Fe attempted to have a network of rail lines that reached to the Pacific Southwest, the Pacific Northwest, and northern California; only the Union Pacific succeeded. The American rail network was essentially complete by 1910 when the last transcontinental line, the Western Pacific Railroad to Oakland, Calif., was opened.

ADVANCES IN TRACTION SYSTEMS

Diesel-electric locomotives appeared in the 1920s. Individual locomotive units provided up to 5,000 horsepower, a figure equal to all the steam-engine power in the United States in 1800. Locomotive units could be multicoupled and operated by a single engineer. It became routine to run "unit trains" containing 100 to 150 freight cars, semipermanently coupled together and operating over a single long run carrying a single commodity, most commonly coal but also other minerals or grains. Not only did diesel-electric locomotives make such routinization of freight operation possible but they also reduced labour demands greatly. Refueling engines required only pumping heavy fuel oil at infrequent intervals; locomotives frequently ran coast-to-coast with only changes of crew and refueling.

In the first third of the 20th century electrification of standard railroads (which came first on the B&O in 1895) proceeded. Never as widespread as in Europe, electrification today is particularly associated with the northeastern United States. This regional concentration of electrification has meant that only between Boston and Washington, D.C., where the federally assembled Amtrak system owns the infrastructure, is there potential to seek easy high-speed rail development. Experimental high-speed projects began in this northeast corridor in the 1960s when both the Pennsylvania Railroad with its electrically operated Metroliners and the New Haven Railroad diesel-electric Turbotrains began running, and since 2000 Amtrak has run its electric Acela Express trains between Boston and Washington. The Metroliners (phased out in 2006) attained speeds of 125 miles (200 km) per hour in the best sections, while the Acela Express trains are capable of reaching speeds in excess of 150 miles (240 km) per hour (though average operating speeds over the entire route are far lower, generally about 75 miles, or 120 km, per hour).

RAILWAY COMPANY MERGERS

Throughout the 20th century the ownership and organization of U.S. railroads changed. Mergers were common, and the bankruptcy of Penn Central Railroad in 1970 became the nucleus around which a number of northeastern railroads were joined into a nationally owned Consolidated Rail Corporation (Conrail), established by the federal government under the Regional Rail Reorganization Act of 1973. The new company's tracks extended from the Atlantic Ocean to St. Louis and from the Ohio River north to Canada. Although it was set up to be an independent profit-making corporation, in its early years, even with the aid of federal loans, it lost more than the bankrupt lines had lost before consolidation. In 1981 Conrail turned a profit for the first time, and in 1987 the government put its stock up for sale to the public. After several years of profitable operation, the assets of the company were purchased in the late 1990s by two other rail companies, CSX Corporation and Norfolk Southern Corporation.

Conrail locomotives sit idle in a South Philadelphia yard in front of a coal-loading pier in 1992. © AP Images

Within months after the Penn Central bankruptcy, a number of railroads applied for Interstate Commerce Commission permission to abandon intercity passenger service. From about the early 1960s, the railroads had lost millions of dollars annually on their passenger lines as a result of a steady decline in their ridership and increases in their operating costs. In 1950, for example, there were approximately 9,000 passenger trains in service, and these lines carried just under 50 percent of all intercity traffic. By 1970, however, there were only about 450 trains still in operation, with a total share of the passenger traffic amounting to a mere 7 percent. Freight service was still modestly profitable, but passenger service was, as virtually everywhere else in the world, possible only with substantial government subsidies. At this point Congress founded the National Railroad Passenger Corporation, or Amtrak, which in 1971 assumed control of passenger service from the nation's private rail companies. More than a century earlier, land grants had been given to railroads to spur completion of the transcontinental line, but the creation of Amtrak marked the first time that rail passenger service received any form of direct financial assistance from the U.S. government. The new corporation was set up to pay the railroads to run their passenger trains and also compensate them for the use of certain facilities, including tracks and terminals. It bore all administrative costs, such as those incurred for the purchase of new equipment, and managed scheduling, route planning, and the sale of tickets. Income from passenger fares has never been sufficient to pay for operating and capital-improvement costs, and as a result Amtrak has regularly received subsidies from the federal government—in addition to constant scrutiny of its operating and budgetary practices and periodic threats from Congress to reduce or even eliminate funding.

By the turn of the 21st century, rail was estimated to account for only about 1 percent of intercity traffic in the United States. Amtrak was responsible for some 21,000 miles (34,000 km) of track around the country, though by far most of its ridership was found in so-called urban corridors, short- or medium-distance routes that linked centres of high population. The Northeast Corridor in particular became Amtrak's most important service area. In this megalopolis, extending roughly from Boston through New York City to Washington, D.C., the dense population presented a market that could be exploited by a fast modern rail passenger service. In 1976 Amtrak took over the route, assuming direct ownership of the tracks and facilities. At the same time, a federally funded Northeast Corridor Improvement Project was begun to upgrade the route for high speed and extend electrification over the entire route. By 1991 the route between

New York and Washington could be run at high speed by Metroliner trains, which were hauled by lightweight, 7,000-horsepower electric locomotives of Swedish design. The Metroliner was replaced between 2000 and 2006 by the Acela Express, whose passenger cars and electric power cars were built by Bombardier Inc., a Montreal-based builder of aircraft and transportation equipment, in partnership with the French company Alstom, a manufacturer of electric motors and other power equipment. In the face of severe airline shuttle competition, Amtrak's frequent train service has become the dominant public passenger carrier in the New York–Washington corridor. In 2010 Amtrak claimed more than one-half of the combined rail and air passenger market between those two cities and also between New York and Boston.

CANADIAN RAILROADS

In its earliest years Canadian railroading was influenced by British rail practice, but after a decade of experience with North American economic and geographic realities, American practice began a fairly rapid rise to dominance that has remained to the present. The first transborder line was completed between Portland, Maine, and Montreal in 1852; it was known as the Atlantic and St. Lawrence Railroad in the three northern New England states and the St. Lawrence and Atlantic in Quebec. At the behest of the Maine promoters of this line a gauge of 5 feet 6 inches (1,676 mm) was adopted to exclude Boston and its standard-gauge railroads from participation. Once the railroad opened, the international company was sold to and extended by a British company, the Grand Trunk Railway, which ultimately constructed a line from Rivière-du-Loup on the St. Lawrence estuary below Quebec city to Sarnia on the St. Clair River at the Ontario-Michigan

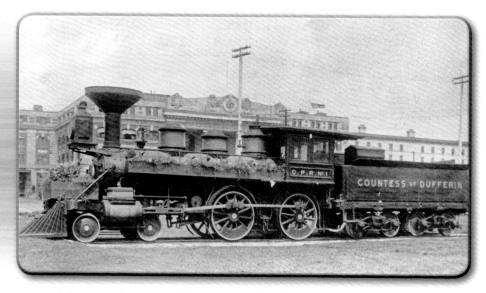

The steam locomotive Countess of Dufferin, *built by the Baldwin Locomotive Works of Philadelphia in 1872 for the Northern Pacific Railway and sold in 1877 to the Canadian Pacific Railway.* Encyclopædia Britannica, Inc.

frontier. The Grand Trunk infrastructure was much more costly than that found on any other rail line in North America following British practice but was laid out on the Maine gauge of 5 feet 6 inches, which became the first widely adopted Canadian gauge. Only later when the rail crossings of the international boundary became numerous and the generally unsatisfactory example of the Grand Trunk was fully understood were the broad Canadian lines narrowed to the standard gauge.

The Canadian Shield posed a serious obstacle to transcontinental planning. British Columbia, then a British crown colony, was concerned about the impact of an influx of gold prospectors from the United States, and it sought to join the Canadian confederation. In 1871 Prime Minister John A. Macdonald offered British Columbia a railroad connection with the Canadian network within 10 years.

An agreement was reached with little knowledge of where and how such a rail line could be built. A Canadian Pacific Railway survey was begun under the direction of Sandford Fleming, former chief engineer of the Intercolonial Railway in the Maritime Provinces. There was some question as to the best route across the Canadian Shield from Callender in eastern Ontario (then the head of steel production in eastern Canada) to the edge of the prairies in eastern Manitoba, but simplicity of construction favoured the northern shore of Lake Superior. In the prairies the choice seemed to rest on which pass through the Rockies would be used. Fleming strongly favoured Yellowhead Pass near present-day Jasper, but the rail builders chose instead Kicking Horse Pass west of Calgary because it would place the railroad much closer to the 49th parallel, thus shielding business in western Canada from competition with American railroads. The final question to be resolved by the Fleming Survey was the route to be employed across the Coast Ranges of British Columbia. Five routes ranging between the Fraser River valley in the south and the Skeena River near the 54th parallel in the north were considered, but the Fraser gorge route to the mouth of that river was selected. By 1885, when the Canadian Pacific Railway (CP) was completed by a joining of tracks at Craigellachie in British Columbia, Burrard Inlet, north of the Fraser mouth, was selected as a new port and was named for George Vancouver, the British naval captain who conducted the most detailed survey of this coast.

The CP tied the recently formed dominion together but operated on such a thin market that its charges were high and its network of lines limited. In Manitoba at the turn of the 20th century wheat farmers sought more rail lines, and the province encouraged ramification of the lines with land grants. By the end of the first decade of the century one granger road, the Canadian Northern

Labourers employed by Canadian railroad contractor Andrew Onderdonk laying track in the lower Fraser valley, B.C., Can., 1883. CP Rail Corporate Archives

Railway, promoted a line from Montreal to Winnipeg and then, along with its network of prairie railroads, a second rail route to the Pacific coast, using Yellowhead Pass. This second transcontinental line was finished during World War I, though wartime inflation led to bankruptcy for its promoters.

In the first decade of the 20th century a third transcontinental line was advanced rapidly through a large government subsidy. A proposal was made to construct a rail line from Moncton, N.B., near the ports of Halifax and Saint John, passing through mainly timbered land to the south bank of the St. Lawrence River at Levis opposite Quebec city. From there, the National Transcontinental Railway crossed the Canadian Shield to Winnipeg. There the project was joined to a line of the Grand Trunk. The Grand Trunk Pacific Railway beginning at Winnipeg passed through the fertile belt of the prairies to Edmonton, continuing thence to Yellowhead Pass and across central British Columbia to a totally new port on Kaien Island in Canada just south of the Alaska Panhandle, which was named Prince Rupert. Unfortunately the addition of two new transcontinentals within little more than a year in a time of great inflation placed both concerns in bankruptcy and led to their reversion to public ownership as the Canadian National Railways (CN) in 1918.

Since then, there have been further demands for rail lines in Canada, mostly to gain access to heavy raw materials. Manitoba shaped a new port at Churchill on Hudson Bay at the end of the 1920s. Lines from the north shore of the Gulf of St. Lawrence were pushed into Labrador to reach iron deposits in the 1950s. Access to lead-zinc deposits near Great Slave Lake brought a "railway to resources" at Hay River in the Northwest Territory. British Columbia took over an initially private company, the Pacific Great

Eastern Railway, and shaped it into the British Columbia Railway. Even the CN has reflected this increasing focus on resource flows. In 1989 it opened the Mount MacDonald Tunnel, the longest tunnel in the Western Hemisphere at just over 9 miles (14.5 km); it runs under Rogers Pass in the Selkirk Range of British Columbia. This reflects the turn-about in rail flows in Canada, where transpacific shipping has overtaken transatlantic routes. The steep grades in Rogers Pass required huge horsepower in helper (pusher) engines. By tunneling beneath Mount Macdonald, the transit of the Selkirks was flattened to just under 1 percent.

Despite the fact that Canada's railways have served for 150 years as Canada's spine, linking the scattered former British colonies into a single transcontinental country, the system faces challenges in the 21st century. The most important concern is rail-passenger service, which fell off dramatically in the decades after World War II owing to competition from airplanes and automobiles. Much of the rolling stock became outdated, leading to inefficient and costly service. In 1978 the Canadian government established VIA Rail Canada, Inc., as a crown corporation independent of the CN and CP to assume full responsibility for managing all the country's rail-passenger services (except for commuter lines and some small local lines). VIA was formed in the hope that it would permit an economy of scale not possible when the CN and CP railroads ran independent passenger services, thereby reducing the subsidies needed to support Canada's rail-passenger system. Unfortunately, the new company acquired ownership of all CN and CP passenger locomotives but did not purchase any track; instead, it compensates the railroads for the cost of operating VIA trains over their tracks. This has only aggravated a perennial problem of arriving at a government subsidy sufficient to meet the service's

THE CANADIAN NATIONAL RAILWAY COMPANY

CN is a corporation created by the Canadian government in 1918 to operate a number of nationalized railroads (including the old Grand Trunk lines, the Intercolonial Railway, the National Transcontinental Railway, and the Canadian Northern Railway) as one of Canada's two transcontinental railroad systems. Headquarters are in Montreal.

In its early years Canadian National engaged in a fierce competitive struggle with the privately owned Canadian Pacific Railway Ltd. This ended with the Canadian National–Canadian Pacific Act in 1933, which directed the railways to cooperate by eliminating duplication of services. In 1978 Canadian National's passenger services were taken over by VIA Rail Canada. In 1995, in what was at the time the largest privatization in Canadian history, the government sold off its stock in CN. Four years later the railroad acquired all the stock of the Illinois Central Railroad, thereby forming a rail network that reached from the Gulf of Mexico to the Atlantic and Pacific coasts of Canada. In 1998 an alliance with Kansas City Southern Railway extended CN's lines into Mexico, fully realizing CN's goal of becoming "the NAFTA railroad," establishing itself as an important carrier of freight between Canada, the United States, and Mexico under the terms of the North American Free Trade Agreement.

Canadian National's transcontinental line extends from several cities on Canada's east coast to Vancouver and Prince Rupert, B.C., in the west. CN ships coal, forest products (including lumber and newsprint), chemicals, petroleum products, automotive parts and products, and agricultural goods. In 1973–75 the company built Toronto's CN Tower (opened 1976), which remained the world's tallest freestanding structure until 2007. Ownership of the CN Tower transferred to the Canadian government in 1995 as part of a streamlining of the company before privatization.

operating budget and also to fund fleet modernization, track improvements, and other capital developments.

If the future of rail transportation in central Canada is uncertain, Canada's north has seen an interesting transition as railways originally built to open the frontier have turned to providing spectacularly scenic journeys for vacationers. In the west, successors to the original trans-continental routes—the Rocky Mountaineer through Banff and the Canadian through Jasper—wind among the majestic Rocky Mountains. From Winnipeg a railway passes through rugged lake and forest country to reach the ocean port of Churchill on Hudson Bay. Ontario's two northern lines are the Algoma Central, which runs from Sault Ste. Marie through the Agawa Canyon, resplendent with hardwoods in the fall, and the Northland, which cuts through the mineral-rich Canadian Shield to Moosonee, close to an old fur-trading post on James Bay. In Quebec, the line running north from the Gulf of St. Lawrence to the iron-ore deposits of Ungava and Labrador is used to bring canoeists, fishermen, and hunters into the last great wilderness region of eastern North America.

MODERN RAILWAYS AROUND THE WORLD

With the 20th century the railroad reached maturity. Railroad building continued on a fairly extensive scale in some parts of the world, notably in Canada, China, the Soviet Union, and Africa. But in most of the more developed countries construction tapered off until the second half of the century. Then it was revived, first by the demand for new urban transit railroads or the expansion of existing systems and, from 1970 onward, by the creation in Europe and East Asia of new high-speed inter-city passenger lines. The technological emphasis shifted to faster operations, more amenities for passengers, larger and more specialized freight cars, safer and more sophisti-cated signaling and traffic-control systems, and new types of motive power. Railroads in many of the more advanced countries also found themselves operating in a new climate of intense competition with other forms of transport.

DIESEL-ELECTRIC LOCOMOTION AND ELECTRONIC SYSTEMS

In the first half of the 20th century, advances in railroad technology and operating practice were limited. One of the most far-reaching was the perfection of diesel traction as a more efficient alternative to steam and as a more cost-effective option than electrification where train movements were not intensive. Another was the move from mechanical signaling and telephonic traffic-control methods to electrical systems that enabled centralized control of considerable traffic areas. Also significant was the first use of continuously welded rail, a major contribution to improved vehicle riding and to longer track life and reduced maintenance costs.

From roughly 1960 onward the developed world's railroads, pressed hard by highway and air competition, progressed swiftly into a new technological age. Steam traction had been eliminated from North America and disappeared from western Europe's national railroads when British Railways dispensed with it in 1968. In China the world's only remaining steam locomotive factory switched to electric locomotive manufacture in 1991. Diesel-electric traction had become far more reliable and cheaper to run, though electric traction's performance characteristics and operating costs were superior. But up to mid-century only high-traffic routes could optimize electric traction's economy, not least because of the heavy capital cost of the fixed works required to set up the traction current supply system.

In the second half of the century, new technology achieved a steady reduction in electrification's initial cost and a rapid advance in electric traction's power and performance relative to locomotive size and weight. Particularly influential on both counts was the successful French pioneering of electrification with a direct supply of high-voltage alternating current at the industrial frequency. This stimulated particularly large electrification programs in China, Japan, South Korea, some eastern European countries, and India in particular. Those railroads already electrified to a considerable extent either kept their existing system or, with the perfection of locomotives able to work with up to four different types of traction voltage—whether alternating or direct current—adopted the high-voltage system for new electrification. Another stimulus for electrification came with the sharp rise in oil prices and the realization of the risks of dependence on imported oil as fuel that followed the 1973 Middle East crisis. Today only a minority of western European trunk rail routes are still worked by diesel traction.

Few industries stood to benefit more than the railroads from the rapid advances in electronics, which found a wealth of applications from real-time operations monitoring and customer services to computer-based traffic control. The potential of solid-state devices for miniaturizing and enhancing on-board components was another key factor in electric traction development.

The latest technologies were deployed in the integrated design of high-performance track and vehicles, both freight and passenger, and for development of high-speed passenger systems to challenge air transport and the huge growth of private auto travel over improved national highways. Intermodal techniques were developed to keep a rail component in the trunk haul of high-rated freight, the source or destination of which could no longer be directly rail-served economically. The cost of maintaining high-quality track was reduced by the emergence of a wide range of mobile machinery capable of every task, from complete renewal of a length of line to ballast cleaning or packing, ultrasonic rail flaw detection, and electronic checking of track alignment.

GROWTH IN DEVELOPING COUNTRIES

At the same time, new trunk route construction was considerable in the developing countries, where increasing route capacity was essential for bulk movement of raw materials to expanding industries and to foster regional socioeconomic development. India's rail system, with some 39,000 miles (63,000 km) of track length, is one of the most extensive in the world, while in terms of the distance travelled each year by passengers it is the world's most heavily used system. (India's mountain railways were

A 1905 model steam engine running on the Shimla-Kalka Railway Line in Shimla, India. © AP Images

collectively designated a UNESCO World Heritage site in 2008.) There has been conversion to double-track lines, as well as a shift from steam locomotives to diesel-electric or electric power.

Between 1950 and 1990 China doubled the route-length of its national system to some 33,500 miles (54,000 km), and between 1990 and 2010 it doubled its route-length again, to approximately 66,000 miles (110,000 km). China's rail network is now the longest in the world. Since the late 1950s there has been a change in railway-construction policy. Prior to that time, most attention was paid to the needs of the eastern half of China, where most of the coal network is found; since then, more emphasis has been given to extending the rail system into the western provinces. These projects, which have been coordinated on a national level, contrast to the pattern prevailing before World War II, when foreign-financed railroads were built in different places without any attempt to coordinate or standardize the transport and communications system. Since 1990 great effort has been made not only to speed up new construction but also to improve the original railway system, including such measures as building bridges, laying double tracks, and using continuous welded rail. In addition, important rail links have been electrified, and high-speed passenger rail service is being installed.

HIGH-SPEED PASSENGER LINES

Even as the automobile and airplane have risen to prominence, railroads have developed the technologies to compete with them in the vital intercity market. It is now well within the capabilities of train manufacturers and railway operators to provide equipment and service that will transport passengers over long distances at speeds averaging 125 miles (200 km) per hour or more. Indeed, on many high-speed rail lines, average service speeds faster than 185 miles (300 km) per hour are not uncommon. In April 2007, a special Train à Grande Vitesse (TGV), the high-speed train run by the French National Railways, set a speed record of 357.2 miles (574.8 km) per hour on a test track in northern France. In some parts of Europe and East Asia, where high-speed rail service has made it possible to reach once-distant destinations in only a few hours, passengers have begun to move away from air and road travel. This movement is highly desired by some economic planners for the benefits it brings in reducing consumption of fossil fuels, lowering emission of pollutants, and relieving congestion on highways and at airports.

JAPAN

Construction of new railroads for high-speed passenger trains was pioneered by Japan. In 1957 a government study concluded that the existing line between Tokyo and Ōsaka, built to the historic Japanese track gauge of 3 feet 6 inches (1,067 mm), was incapable of upgrading to the needs of the densely populated and industrialized Tōkaidō coastal belt between the two cities. In April 1959 work began on a standard 4-feet-8.5-inch (1,435-mm), 320-mile (515-km) Tokyo-Ōsaka railway engineered for the exclusive use of streamlined electric passenger trains. Opened in October 1964, this first Shinkansen (Japanese: "New Trunk Line") was an immediate commercial success. By March 1975 it had been extended via a tunnel under the Kammon-Kaikyo Strait to Hakata in Kyushu island, to complete a 664-mile (1,068-km) high-speed route from Tokyo. Other lines radiating northward from Tokyo were completed in 1982 to the cities of Niigata (the Jōetsu line) and Morioka (the Tōhoku line). The Tōhoku line subsequently was extended northward to Hachinohe in 2002 and on to Aomori in 2010. Branches from the Tōhoku line to Yamagata opened in 1992 and to Akita in 1997; a branch from the Jōetsu line to Nagano also opened in 1997. Segments of a further extension of the Nagano branch westward to Toyama and Kanazawa have been under construction since the early 1990s. In addition, a line was completed between Yatsushiro and Kagoshima in southwestern Kyushu in 2004; work has been underway since the late 1990s to extend that line northward from Yatsushiro to Hakata.

The Japanese "bullet trains" initially ran at a top speed of 130 miles (210 km) per hour, but speeds have steadily been raised in order to compete with growing passenger air transport. The Hayabusa ("Falcon") train, introduced on the Tōhoku line in 2011, is capable of reaching 185 miles (300 km) per hour.

WESTERN EUROPE

Except for its automatic speed-control signaling system, the first Shinkansen was essentially a derivation of the traction, vehicle, and infrastructure technology of the 1960s. France's first high-speed, or Train à Grande Vitesse (TGV), line from Paris to Lyon, partially opened in September 1981 and commissioned throughout in October 1983, was the product of integrated infrastructure and train design based on more than two decades of research. Dedication of the new line to a single type of high-powered, lightweight train-set (a permanently coupled, invariable set of vehicles with inbuilt traction) enabled engineering of the infrastructure with gradients as steep as 3.5 percent, thereby minimizing earthwork costs, without detriment to maintenance of a 168-mile-(270-km-) per hour maximum speed. A second high-speed line, the TGV-Atlantique, from Paris to junctions near Le Mans and Tours with existing main lines serving western France, was opened in 1989–90. This was built with slightly easier ruling gradients, allowing maximum operating speed to be raised to 185 miles (300 km) per hour.

France went on to construct more lines under a master plan that would extend TGV service from Paris to all major French cities, interconnect key provincial centres, and plug the French TGV network into the high-speed systems emerging in neighbouring countries. The latter included Britain, to which a rail tunnel under the English Channel was opened in 1994. The tunnel railway, known as Eurostar, has directly connected Paris and London on a dedicated line since 2007; travel time between the two cities is 2 hours 15 minutes, making the service directly competitive with airlines. Eurostar also travels between London and Brussels in less than two hours by connecting to a TGV route between Paris and Brussels. Since 2009 the Netherlands has connected its western group of cities with the Paris-London-Brussels high-speed triangle.

In 1991 Germany completed new Hannover-Würzburg and Mannheim-Stuttgart lines engineered to carry both passenger trains at 174 miles (280 km) per hour and merchandise freight trains at 100 miles (160 km) per hour. This was the beginning of Germany's InterCity Express (ICE) high-speed rail network, which has continued to grow as further lines have been constructed, notably between Hannover and Berlin (opened 1998) and in Germany's most heavily trafficked corridor, Cologne–Frankfurt am Main (opened 2002).

In Italy the first Alta Velocità (AV; "High-Speed") line, running the 150 miles (250 km) from Rome to Florence and designed for 185-mile- (300-km-) per hour top speed, was finished in 1992; the first segment had been opened in 1977, but progress thereafter had been hampered by funding uncertainties and severe geologic problems encountered in the project's tunneling. After some controversy over finance, the line was extended north from

Florence to Milan and then Turin and south from Rome to Naples, the last links in these extensions being opened in 2009. Construction continues on a high-speed west-east route from Turin through Milan and Verona to Venice.

In 1992 Spain completed a new line, the Alta Velocidad Española (AVE; "Spanish High-Speed"), between Madrid and Sevilla (Seville), built not to the country's traditional broad 5-feet-6-inch (1,676-mm) gauge but to the European standard of 4 feet 8.5 inches (1,435 mm). Other routes from Madrid followed, running to Valladolid in 2007, Barcelona in 2008, and Valencia in 2010. The first AVE trains were of French TGV design, built by the Alstom company, but other trains have been based on German ICE designs built by Siemens and on a Spanish design built by the Spanish company Talgo and a division of the Canadian company Bombardier. The AVE, capable of top speeds higher than 185 miles (300 km) per hour, makes the 370-mile (600-km) journey from Madrid to Barcelona in less than three hours, cutting normal train travel time in half and directly competing with air travel.

European high-speed systems such as those outlined above have been authorized and financed separately by each country. However, there has been a simultaneous trend toward a common set of standards—for instance, in track gauge, electric power, and signaling—that points toward a fully integrated European high-speed rail network in the future. The beginning of this network has been seen in limited high-speed service between France, Germany, and the Benelux countries Belgium and the Netherlands. The inclusion of countries such as Spain and Italy, which are separated from their European neighbours by formidable mountain chains, will require the completion not only of ambitious plans to lay new track and build new trains but also of projects to drill tunnels and build viaducts capable of supporting high-speed trains.

SOUTH KOREA, TAIWAN, AND CHINA

Outside Europe, the countries of South Korea, Taiwan, and China are firmly committed to construction of high-speed passenger lines. In South Korea a major line, some 240 miles (400 km) long, is planned to run between the capital, Seoul, and the southern port of Pusan. The first phase, from Seoul to Taegu, began service in 2004, and the second phase, from Taegu to Pusan, is to be completed by 2015. The Korean system employs trains based on French TGV designs. In Taiwan the main high-speed line, running approximately 210 miles (350 km) between the capital, Taipei, and the major port of Kao-hsiung, opened in 2007. The trains are Japanese designs, based on the Shinkansen.

The Chinese high-speed rail network dwarfs those of its Asian neighbours and in fact has become the largest in the world. In 2010 there were some 3,000 miles (5,000 km) of rail dedicated to high-speed trains, and the Chinese government was engaged in a huge public-works program to increase the high-speed network to more than 9,000 miles (15,000 km) by 2020—a total length that would give China more high-speed rail than the rest of the world combined. China's high-speed system is two-tiered. The lower tier is made up of trains that run at 125–150 miles (200–250 km) per hour on track also used by normal passenger and freight trains, and in the upper tier are very high-speed trains running at speeds up to 215 miles (350 km) per hour on dedicated track. Very high-speed lines range from a short 70-mile (115-km) line linking the capital city of Beijing with the northern port of Tianjin, which opened in 2008, to an 800-mile (1,300-km) line between Beijing and the port of Shanghai, and was inaugurated in 2011. Another ambitious long-distance line runs 600 miles (1,000 km) between the industrial city of Wuhan and the major southern port of Guangzhou (Canton).

The Wuhan-Guangzhou line is being extended northward 660 miles (1,100 km) to Beijing, with the goal of completing a monumental high-speed line of more than 1,200 miles (2,000 km) between Guangzhou and the capital. Other ambitious long-distance high-speed lines are being built between the eastern and western parts of the country. The first high-speed trains were Japanese and European designs, built in joint ventures between Chinese and foreign companies, but in subsequent trains Chinese manufacturers transferred foreign technologies to their own designs.

NORTH AMERICA

Since the 1970s various schemes for high-speed rail have been advanced in the United States, though widely separated population centres and relatively low fossil-fuel costs have tended to make politicians more willing to subsidize highway and air travel than rail travel. In 2009 the federal government proposed to spend billions of dollars on 10 high-speed rail projects that had long been in various stages of study. These included lines in California (from Sacramento to San Diego), Florida (from Tampa to Orlando and then Miami), the Midwest (with Chicago serving as a "hub" from which lines would radiate to cities such as Detroit, Mich.; Cincinnati, Ohio; St. Louis, Mo.; and Minneapolis-St. Paul, Minn.), and the Northeast Corridor (where track and other infrastructure would be improved to allow existing service to approach true high speeds). Of the proposals for new construction, the most likely one was a line that would extend from Sacramento, the capital of California, 800 miles (1,300 km) south through San Francisco and Los Angeles to San Diego, close to the border with Mexico—though even then the first major portion, between San Francisco and Los Angeles, would not be finished before 2020. Some state authorities refused to participate in the projects, insisting that in the long run their states would have to spend more money than the lines would be worth in terms of job creation, pollution and traffic reduction, and passenger use.

In Canada one perennial concern is to find a way for railways to meet the mounting needs of passenger movement in the 820-mile (1,320-km) central corridor that extends from Quebec City in the east through Montreal, Ottawa, and Toronto to Windsor in the west—an area that contains more than half of Canada's population. Several proposals have been made for turning over traffic in the corridor to a high-speed line similar to those of Europe or the northeastern United States.

MAGLEV

As an alternative to high-speed rail based on traditional flanged-wheel vehicles, the technology of magnetic levitation, or maglev, has received considerable attention and research, though its practical applications have been limited by cost, safety concerns, and satisfaction with traditional high-speed systems. A maglev vehicle rides on an air cushion created by electromagnetic reaction between an on-board device and another embedded in its guideway. Propulsion and braking are achieved by varying the frequency and voltage of a linear motor system embodied in the guideway and reacting with magnets on the vehicles. Two systems have been developed, one in Germany and the other in Japan. The German system, known as Transrapid, achieves levitation by magnetic attraction; deep skirtings on its vehicles, wrapping around the outer rims of the guideway, contain levitation and guidance electromagnets that, when energized, are attracted to ferromagnetic armature rails at the guideway's extremities and lift the vehicle. The Japanese technology is based on the magnetic repulsion of high-power, helium-cooled

JAPAN'S BULLET TRAIN

Originally built and operated by the government-owned Japanese National Railways, the high-speed Shinkansen ("New Trunk Line") has been part of the private Japan Railways Group since 1987. The first section of the original line, a 320-mile (515-km) stretch between Tokyo and Ōsaka, was opened in 1964. Known as the New Tōkaidō Line, it generally follows and is named for the historic and celebrated Tōkaidō ("Eastern Sea Road") highway that was used especially during the Tokugawa (Edo) period (1603–1867). Many extensions and branchlines have been built since then.

Much of the Shinkansen's track runs through tunnels, including one under Shimonoseki Strait between Honshu and Kyushu and another on the Tokyo-Niigata line that is 14 miles (23 km) long. Several hundred trains operate daily on the system. The most frequent service is between Tokyo and Ōsaka, especially during the morning and evening rush hours, when trains depart at intervals of 10 minutes or less. The fastest trains can make the trip from Tokyo to Hakata in about 5 hours. The electric, multiple-unit trains, which can seat 1,000 passengers or more, derive their power from an overhead wire system. Improvements in track, train cars, and other components have made possible top speeds of between 150 and 185 miles (240 and 300 km) per hour. Such high speeds have made it necessary to develop elaborate safety features. Each car, for example, is equipped with brakes consisting of cast-iron disks and metallic pad linings specially designed not to distort under emergency braking. Moreover, all movements of the trains are monitored and controlled by a central computerized facility in Tokyo.

superconductor magnets on the vehicle and coils of the same polarity in the guideway. On a test track in Japan, a three-car manned train using this technology attained a speed of 361 miles (581 km) per hour in 2003.

The technology has struggled to find practical application, however. In 1984 maglev was applied in Britain to a short-distance, fully automated, low-speed shuttle moving people the 650 yards (600 metres) between Birmingham's airport and a nearby intercity rail station. The shuttle was replaced in 1995 by a cheaper cable system. Only in China is there a commercially operating high-speed maglev line—also an airport shuttle, ferrying passengers between Shanghai's Pudong International Airport and the city centre. The Shanghai system, based on the German maglev model, makes the 18-mile (30-km) trip in eight minutes. For the creation of high-speed intercity maglev routes, however, political support is consistently lacking. A proposal to extend the Shanghai line 120 miles (200 km) to Hangzhou failed in the face of competition from traditional high-speed technology, Even in Germany, one of the home countries of maglev technology, a proposed 240-mile (400-km) line between Hamburg and Berlin and even a 22-mile (35-km) shuttle between the Cologne and Düsseldorf airports failed to gain support. In Japan, the Central Japan Railway Company has proposed construction of a 270-mile (450-km) maglev line connecting Tokyo and Ōsaka to relieve the overtaxed Shinkansen between those two cities, but this service would not open until after 2025.

Routinely, estimates submitted for construction of maglev intercity lines, which would require an elevated guideway, indicate the projects would be more expensive per kilometre than a new high-speed wheel-on-rail line between the same points. In Europe, many new high-speed wheel-on-rail lines are compatible with traditional railroads, so high-speed trains can often freely range beyond the limits of their new lines. A maglev line would be completely incompatible; to adopt maglev could be the start of duplicating existing rail intercity networks, which in light of rapid advances in conventional rail speed would be economically illogical.

CHAPTER 3

LOCOMOTIVES

Although motive power for a train-set can be incorporated into a car that also has passenger, baggage, or freight accommodations, it most often is provided by a separate unit, the locomotive, which includes the machinery to generate (or, in the case of an electric locomotive, to convert) power and transmit it to the driving wheels. Today there are two main sources of power for a locomotive: oil (in the form of diesel fuel) and electricity. Steam, the earliest form of propulsion, was in almost universal use until about the time of World War II; since then it has been superseded by the more efficient diesel and electric traction.

The steam locomotive was a self-sufficient unit, carrying its own water supply for generating the steam and coal, oil, or wood for heating the boiler. The diesel locomotive also carries its own fuel supply, but the diesel-engine output cannot be coupled directly to the wheels; instead, a mechanical, electric, or hydraulic transmission must be used. The electric locomotive is not self-sufficient; it picks up current from an overhead wire or a third rail beside the running rails. (Third-rail supply is employed only by urban rapid-transit railroads operating on low-voltage direct current.)

In the 1950s and '60s the gas turbine was adopted by one American and some European railroads as an alternative to the diesel engine. Although its advantages have been nullified by advances in diesel traction technology and increases in oil price, it is still proposed as an alternative means for installing high-speed rail service for regions where no infrastructure for electric power is in place.

STEAM LOCOMOTIVES

The basic features that made George and Robert Stephenson's *Rocket* of 1829 successful—its multitube boiler and its system of exhausting the steam and creating a draft in its firebox—continued to be used in the steam locomotive to the end of its career. The number of coupled drive wheels soon increased. The *Rocket* had only a single pair of driving wheels, but four coupled wheels soon became common, and eventually some locomotives were built with as many as 14 coupled drivers.

Steam-locomotive driving wheels were of various sizes, usually larger for the faster passenger engines. The average was about a 72- to 80-inch (1,829- to 2,032-mm) diameter for passenger engines and 54 to 66 inches (1,372 to 1,676 mm) for freight or mixed-traffic types.

Supplies of fuel (usually coal but sometimes oil) and water could be carried on the locomotive frame itself (in which case it was called a tank engine) or in a separate vehicle, the tender, coupled to the locomotive. The tender of a typical European main-line locomotive had a capacity of 10 tons (9,000 kg) of coal and 8,000 gallons (30,000 litres) of water. In North America, higher capacities were common.

To meet the special needs of heavy freight traffic in some countries, notably the United States, greater tractive effort was obtained by using two separate engine units under a common boiler. The front engine was articulated, or hinge-connected to the frame of the rear engine so that the very large locomotive could negotiate curves. The articulated locomotive was originally a Swiss invention, with the first built in 1888. The largest ever built was the Union Pacific's *Big Boy*, used in mountain freight service in the western United States. *Big Boy* weighed more than 600 short tons, including the tender. It could exert 135,400 pounds (61,400 kg) of tractive force and developed more than 6,000 horsepower at 70 miles (112 km) per hour.

One of the best-known articulated designs was the Beyer-Garratt, which had two frames, each having its own driving wheels and cylinders, surmounted by water tanks. Separating the two chassis was another frame carrying the boiler, cab, and fuel supply. This type of locomotive was valuable on lightly laid track; it could also negotiate sharp curves. It was widely used in Africa.

Various refinements gradually improved the reciprocating steam locomotive. Some included higher boiler pressures (up to 290–300 pounds per square inch [2,000–2,060 kilopascals] for some of the last locomotives, compared with about 200 pounds per square inch [1,300 kilopascals] for earlier designs), superheating, feed-water preheating, roller bearings, and the use of poppet (perpendicular) valves rather than sliding piston valves.

Still, the thermal efficiency of even the ultimate steam locomotives seldom exceeded about 6 percent. Incomplete combustion and heat losses from the firebox, boiler, cylinders, and elsewhere dissipated most of the energy of the fuel burned. For this reason the steam locomotive became obsolete, but only slowly, because it had compensating advantages, notably its simplicity and ability to withstand abuse.

ELECTRIC TRACTION

Efforts to propel railroad vehicles using batteries date from 1835, but the first successful application of electric traction was in 1879, when an electric locomotive ran at

BIG BOY

Big Boy was the name given to one of the largest and most powerful series of steam locomotives ever built. Produced by the American Locomotive Company of Schenectady, N.Y., exclusively for the Union Pacific Railroad, it was designed primarily to handle heavy freight traffic in the Wasatch Mountains, where trains faced a continuous grade of 1.55 percent on a stretch of track east of Ogden, Utah.

A *Big Boy* locomotive along with its tender weighed about 604 tons and measured more than 132 feet (40 metres) in length. It had a maximum power capacity of more than 6,000 horsepower and could haul a 3,600-ton train unassisted up the Wasatch Mountain grade. Pulling freight on level track, it could achieve a speed of 70 miles (112 km) per hour.

The *Big Boy* locomotives had an articulated design; the frame of the front engine was hinge-connected to the rear engine under a single boiler. The wheel arrangement was designated 4-8-8-4—i.e., a set of 4 pilot wheels led a set of 8 coupled driving wheels, which were compounded by another set of 8 coupled drivers, with 4 trailing wheels.

Twenty-five *Big Boy*s were produced from 1941 to 1944. They operated almost exclusively in the mountainous region between Cheyenne, Wyo., and Ogden, Utah, their most prominent service being the pulling of long trains loaded with agricultural produce. They were gradually replaced by diesel-electric locomotives; the last one was taken out of regular service in 1959. Preserved *Big Boy* locomotives can be seen today in railroad museums in Cheyenne, Denver, Omaha, St. Louis, and other cities.

an exhibition in Berlin. The first commercial applications of electric traction were for suburban or metropolitan railroads. One of the earliest came in 1895, when the Baltimore and Ohio electrified a stretch of track in Baltimore to avoid smoke and noise problems in a tunnel. One of the first countries to use electric traction for main-line operations was Italy, where a system was inaugurated as early as 1902.

The first electric locomotive, built by the Siemens electric company, 1879.
Encyclopædia Britannica, Inc.

By World War I a number of electrified lines were operating both in Europe and in the United States. Major electrification programs were undertaken after that war in such countries as Sweden, Switzerland, Norway, Germany, and Austria. By the end of the 1920s nearly every European country had at least a small percentage of electrified track. Electric traction also was introduced in Australia (1919), New Zealand (1923), India (1925), Indonesia (1925), and South Africa (1926). A number of metropolitan terminals and suburban services were electrified between 1900 and 1938 in the United States, and there were a few main-line electrifications. The advent of the diesel locomotive inhibited further trunk route electrification in the United States after 1938, but following World War II such electrification was rapidly extended elsewhere. Today a significant percentage of the standard-gauge track in national railroads around the world is electrified—for example, in Japan (100 percent), Switzerland (92 percent), Belgium (91 percent), the Netherlands (76 percent), Spain (76 percent), Italy (68 percent), Sweden (65 percent), Austria (65 percent), Norway (62 percent), South Korea (55 percent), France (52 percent), Germany (48 percent), China (42 percent), and the United Kingdom (32 percent). By contrast, in the United States, which has some 140,000 miles (225,000 km) of standard-gauge track, electrified routes hardly exist outside of the Northeast Corridor, where Amtrak runs the 450-mile (720-km) Acela Express between Boston and Washington, D.C. (In addition, cities worldwide have created many new electrified urban rapid-transit rail systems, as well as extending existing systems.)

ADVANTAGES AND DISADVANTAGES

Electric traction is generally considered the most economical and efficient means of operating a railroad, provided that cheap electricity is available and that the traffic density justifies the heavy capital cost. Being simply power-converting, rather than power-generating, devices, electric locomotives have several advantages. They can draw on the resources of the central power plant to develop power greatly in excess of their nominal ratings to start a heavy train or to surmount a steep grade at high speed. A typical modern electric locomotive rated at 6,000 horsepower has been observed to develop as much as 10,000 horsepower for a short period under these conditions. Moreover, electric locomotives are quieter in operation than other types and produce no smoke or fumes. Electric locomotives require little time in the shop for maintenance, their maintenance costs are low, and they have a longer life than diesels.

The greatest drawbacks to electrified operation are the high capital investment and maintenance cost of the fixed plant—the traction current wires and structures and power substations—and the costly changes that are usually required in signaling systems to immunize their circuitry against interference from the high traction-current voltages and to adapt their performance to the superior acceleration and sustained speeds obtainable from electric traction.

TYPES OF TRACTION SYSTEMS

Electric-traction systems can be broadly divided into those using alternating current and those using direct current. With direct current, the most popular line voltages for overhead wire supply systems have been 1,500 and 3,000. Third-rail systems are predominantly in the 600–750 volt range. The disadvantages of direct current are that expensive substations are required at frequent intervals and the overhead wire or third rail must be relatively large and heavy. The low-voltage, series-wound, direct-current motor is well suited to railroad traction, being simple to construct and easy to control. Until the late 20th century it was universally employed in electric and diesel-electric traction units.

The potential advantages of using alternating instead of direct current prompted early experiments and applications of this system. With alternating current, especially with relatively high overhead-wire voltages (10,000 volts or above), fewer substations are required, and the lighter overhead current supply wire that can be used correspondingly reduces the weight of structures needed to support it, to the further benefit of capital costs of electrification. In the early decades of high-voltage alternating current electrification, available alternating-current motors were not suitable for operation with alternating current of the standard commercial or industrial frequencies (50 hertz [cycles per second] in Europe; 60 hertz in the United States and parts of Japan). It was necessary to use a lower frequency (16 $^2/_3$ hertz is common in Europe; 25 hertz in the United States); this in turn required either special railroad power plants to generate alternating current at the required frequency or frequency-conversion equipment to change the available commercial frequency into the railroad frequency.

Nevertheless, alternating-current supply systems at 16 $^2/_3$ hertz became the standard on several European railroads, such as Austria, Germany, and Switzerland, where electrification began before World War II. Several main-line electrifications in the eastern United States were built using 25-hertz alternating current, which survives in the Northeast Corridor operated by Amtrak.

Interest in using commercial-frequency alternating current in the overhead wire continued, however; and in 1933 experiments were carried out in both Hungary and Germany. The German State Railways electrified its Höllenthal branch at 20,000 volts, 50 hertz.

In 1945 Louis Armand, former president of the French railroads, went ahead with further development of this system and converted a line between Aix-Les-Bains and La Roche-sur-Foron for the first practical experiments. This was so successful that the 25,000-volt, 50- or 60-hertz system has become virtually the standard for new main-line electrification systems.

With commercial-frequency, alternating-current systems, there are two practical ways of taking power to the locomotive driving wheels: (1) by a rotary converter or static rectifier on the locomotive to convert the alternating-current supply into direct current at low voltage to drive standard direct-current traction motors and (2) by a converter system to produce variable-frequency current to drive alternating-current motors. The first method, using nonmechanical rectifiers, was standard practice until the end of the 1970s.

The power-to-weight ratios obtainable with electric traction units had been greatly increased by the end of World War II. Reduction in the bulk of on-board electric apparatus and motors, coupled in the latter with a simultaneous rise in attainable power output, enabled Swiss production for the Bern-Lötschberg-Simplon Railway in 1944 of a 4,000-horsepower locomotive weighing only 80,000 kg (176,370 pounds). Its four axles were all motored. There was no longer need of nonmotorized axles to keep weight on each wheel-set within limits acceptable by the track.

By 1960 the electric industry was producing transformer and rectifier packages slim enough to fit under the frames of a motored urban rapid-transit car, thereby making almost its entire body available for passenger seating. This helped to accelerate and expand the industrialized

An electric locomotive built for the Bern-Lötschberg-Simplon Railway, Switzerland. SSPL via Getty Images

world's electrification of metropolitan railway networks for operation by self-powered train-sets (i.e., with some or all vehicles motored). A virtue of the self-powered train-set principle is its easy adaptation to peaks of traffic demand. When two or more sets are coupled, the additional sets have the extra needed traction power. With both electric and diesel traction it is simple to interconnect electrically the power and braking controls of all the train-sets so that the train they form can be driven from a single cab. Because of this facility such train-sets are widely known as multiple-units. Modern multiple-units are increasingly fitted with automatic couplers that combine a draft function with connection of all power, braking, and other control circuits between two train-sets; this is achieved by automatic engagement, when couplers interlock, of a nest of electric contacts built into each coupler head.

From about 1960 major advances in electric traction accrued from the application of electronics. Particularly significant was the perfection of the semiconductor thyristor, or "chopper," control of current supply to motors. The thyristor—a rapid-action, high-power switch with which the "on" and "off" periods of each cycle can be fractionally varied—achieved smoothly graduated application of voltage to traction motors. Besides eliminating wear-prone parts and greatly improving an electric traction unit's adhesion, thyristor control also reduced current consumption.

Three-phase alternating-current motor traction became practicable in the 1980s. With electronics it was possible to compress to manageable weight and size the complex equipment needed to transmute the overhead wire or third-rail current to a supply of variable voltage and frequency suitable for feeding to three-phase alternating-current motors. For railroad traction the alternating-current motor is preferable to a direct-current machine on several counts. It is an induction motor with a squirrel-cage rotor (that is, solid conductors in the slots are shorted together by end rings), and it has no commutators or brushes and no mechanically contacting parts except bearings, so it is much simpler to maintain and more reliable. It is more compact than a direct motor, so more power is obtainable for a specified motor size and weight; the 14,000-pound (6,000-kg) alternating-current motor in each truck of a modern French National Railways electric locomotive delivers a continuous 3,750 horsepower.

The torque of an alternating-current motor increases with speed, whereas that of a direct-current motor is initially high and falls with rising speed; consequently, the alternating-current motor offers superior adhesion for acceleration of heavy trainloads. Finally, the alternating-current motor is more easily switched into a generating mode to act as a dynamic (rheostatic) or regenerative vehicle brake. (In dynamic braking the current generated to oppose the train's momentum is dissipated through on-board resistances. In regenerative braking, adopted on mountain or intensively operated urban lines where the surplus current can be readily taken up by other trains, it is fed back into the overhead wire or third rail.) The drawbacks of three-phase alternating-current traction are the intricacy of the on-board electrical equipment needed to convert the current supply before it reaches the motors and its higher capital cost by comparison with direct-current motor systems.

A separate traction motor normally serves each axle via a suitably geared drive. For simplicity of final drive it was for many years standard practice to mount the traction motors on a locomotive's axles. As train speeds rose, it became increasingly important to limit the impact on the track of unsprung masses. Now motors are either suspended within a locomotive's trucks or, in the case of some high-speed units, suspended from the locomotive's body and linked to the axles' final drive gearboxes by flexible drive shafts.

The direct-current motor's torque:speed characteristics make a locomotive designed for fast passenger trains, whether electric or diesel-electric, generally unsuitable for freight train work. The heavier loads of the latter require different gearing of the final drives—which will reduce maximum speed—and possibly an increase in the number of motored axles, for increased adhesion. But considerable mixed-traffic haulage capability is obtainable with three-phase alternating-current motors because of their superior adhesion characteristics.

Direct-current motor technology was employed in Japan's first Shinkansen and France's first Paris-Lyon TGV trains, but by the early 1990s three-phase alternating-current traction had been adopted for both Japanese and European very-high-speed train-sets—and by extension the systems around the world that have been derived from them. In Europe, international train operation without a locomotive change at frontiers was complicated by the railways' historic adoption of different electrification systems, either 1,500 or 3,000 volts direct current or 25,000 volts 50 hertz or 15,000 volts 16 ^{2}/$_3$ hertz alternating current. For instance, TGV-type trains could not operate at full efficiency between London, Paris, and Brussels on the Eurostar line via the Channel Tunnel as long as they had to accommodate French 25,000-volt alternating-current overhead wire, Belgian 3,000-volt direct-current overhead wire, and British 750-volt third-rail supply. The French had perfected traction units capable of operating on more than one voltage system soon after they had decided to adopt 25,000-volt alternating-current electrification in areas not wired at their previous 1,500-volt direct current.

Nevertheless, where very-high-speed traction was concerned, it was impossible to contain within acceptable locomotive weight limits the equipment needed for equivalent high-power output under each system. Only after all the new high-speed lines were electrified on high-voltage alternating current was true high-speed service available on the Eurostar line.

Since about 1980 the performance and economy of both electric and diesel traction units have been considerably advanced by the interposition between driving controls and vital components of microprocessors, which ensure that the components respond with maximum efficiency and that they are not inadvertently overtaxed. Another product of the application of electronics to controls is that in the modern electric locomotive the engine operator can set the train speed he wishes to reach or maintain, and the traction equipment will automatically apply or vary the appropriate power to the motors, taking account of train weight and track gradient. The microprocessors also serve a diagnostic function, continuously monitoring the state of the systems they control for signs of incipient or actual fault. The microprocessors are linked to a main on-board computer that instantly reports the nature and location of an actual or potential malfunction to a visual display in the driving cab, generally with advice for the cab crew on how it might be rectified or its effects temporarily mitigated. The cab display also indicates the effectiveness of the countermeasures taken. The computer automatically stores such data, either for downloading to maintenance staff at the journey's end or, on a railroad equipped with train-to-ground-installation radio, for immediate transmission to a maintenance establishment so that preparations for repair of a fault are in place as soon as the traction unit ends its run. In newer very-high-speed, fixed-formation train-sets, a through-train fibre-optics transmission system concentrates data from the microprocessor controls—both those of passenger car systems, such as air-conditioning and power-operated entrance doors, and those of the rear locomotive or, in the Japanese Shinkansen train-sets, the traction equipment dispersed among a proportion of its cars.

DIESEL TRACTION

By the end of the 1960s, diesel had almost completely superseded steam as the standard railroad motive power on nonelectrified lines around the world. The change came first and most quickly in North America, where, during the 25 years from 1935 to 1960 (and especially in the period 1951–60), railroads in the United States completely replaced their steam locomotives.

What caused the diesel to supersede the steam locomotive so rapidly was the pressure of competition from other modes of transport and the continuing rise in wage costs, which forced the railroads to improve their services and adopt every possible measure to increase operating efficiency. Compared with steam, the diesel traction unit had a number of major advantages:

1. It could operate for long periods with no lost time for maintenance; thus, in North America the diesel could operate through on a run of 2,000 miles (3,200 km) or more and then, after servicing, start the return trip. Steam locomotives required extensive servicing after only a few hours' operation.

2. It used less fuel energy than a steam locomotive, for its thermal efficiency was about four times as great.

General Motors' Sound Transit Sounder 902 *passenger commuter diesel powered electric locomotive.* © Transtock/SuperStock

3. It could accelerate a train more rapidly and operate at higher sustained speeds with less damage to the track.

In addition, the diesel was superior to the steam locomotive because of its smoother acceleration, greater cleanliness, standardized repair parts, and operating flexibility (a number of diesel units could be combined and run by one operator under multiple-unit control).

The diesel-electric locomotive is, essentially, an electric locomotive that carries its own power plant. Its use, therefore, brings to a railroad some of the advantages of electrification, but without the capital cost of the power distribution and feed-wire system. As compared with an electric locomotive, however, the diesel-electric has an important drawback: since its output is essentially limited to that of its diesel engine, it can develop less horsepower per locomotive unit. Because high horsepower is required for high-speed operation, the diesel is, therefore, less desirable than the electric for high-speed passenger services and very fast freight operations.

DIESEL DEVELOPMENT

Experiments with diesel-engine locomotives and railcars began almost as soon as the diesel engine was patented by the German engineer Rudolf Diesel in 1892. Attempts at building practical locomotives and railcars (for branch-line passenger runs) continued through the 1920s. The first successful diesel switch engine went into service in 1925; "road" locomotives were delivered to the Canadian National and New York Central railroads in 1928. The first really striking results with diesel traction were obtained in Germany in 1933. There, the *Fliegende Hamburger*, a two-car, streamlined, diesel-electric train, with two 400-horsepower engines, began running between Berlin and Hamburg on a schedule that averaged 77 miles (124 km) per hour. By 1939 most of Germany's principal cities were interconnected by trains of this kind, scheduled to run at average speeds up to 83.3 miles (134.1 km) per hour between stops.

The next step was to build a separate diesel-electric locomotive unit that could haul any train. In 1935 one such unit was delivered to the Baltimore and Ohio and two to the Santa Fe Railway Company. These were passenger units; the first road freight locomotive, a four-unit, 5,400-horsepower Electro-Motive Division, General Motors Corporation demonstrator, was not built until 1939.

By the end of World War II, the diesel locomotive had become a proven, standardized type of motive power, and it rapidly began to supersede the steam locomotive in

North America. In the United States a fleet of 27,000 diesel locomotives proved fully capable of performing more transportation work than the 40,000 steam locomotives they replaced.

After World War II, the use of diesel traction greatly increased throughout the world, though the pace of conversion was generally slower than in the United States.

ELEMENTS OF THE DIESEL LOCOMOTIVE

Although the diesel engine has been vastly improved in power and performance, the basic principles remain the same: drawing air into the cylinder, compressing it so that its temperature is raised, and then injecting a small quantity of oil into the cylinder. The oil ignites without a spark because of the high temperature. The diesel engine may operate on the two-stroke or four-stroke cycle. Rated operating speeds vary from 350 to 2,000 revolutions per minute, and rated output may be from 10 to 4,000 horsepower. Railroads in the United States use engines in the 1,000-revolutions-per-minute range; in Europe and elsewhere, some manufacturers have favoured more compact engines of 1,500–2,000 revolutions per minute.

Most yard-switching and short-haul locomotives are equipped with diesel engines ranging from 600 to 1,800 horsepower; road units commonly have engines ranging from 2,000 to 4,000 horsepower. Most builders use V-type engines, although in-line types are used on smaller locomotives and for underfloor fitment on railcars and multiple-unit train-sets.

The most commonly employed method of power transmission is electric, to convert the mechanical energy produced by the diesel engine to current for electric traction motors. Through most of the 20th century the universal method was to couple the diesel engine to a direct-current generator, from which, through appropriate controls, the current was fed to the motors. Beginning in the 1970s the availability of compact semiconductor rectifiers enabled replacement of the direct-current generator by an alternator, which is able to produce more power and is less costly to maintain than an equivalent direct-current machine. For supply of series-wound direct-current traction motors, static rectifiers converted the three-phase alternating-current output of the alternator to direct current. Then in the 1980s European manufacturers began to adopt the three-phase alternating-current motor for diesel-electric traction units, seeking advantages similar to those obtainable from this technology in electric traction. This requires the direct-current output from the rectifier to be transmuted by a thyristor-controlled inverter into a three-phase variable voltage and frequency supply for the alternating-current motors.

On some railroads with lightly laid track, generally those with narrow rail gauge, locomotives may still need nonmotored as well as motored axles for acceptable weight and bulk distribution. But the great majority of diesel-electric locomotives now have all axles powered.

Other types of transmissions also are used in diesel locomotives. The hydraulic transmission, which first became quite popular in Germany, is often favoured for diesel railcars and multiple-unit train-sets. It employs a centrifugal pump or impeller driving a turbine in a chamber filled with oil or a similar fluid. The pump, driven by the diesel engine, converts the engine power to kinetic energy in the oil impinging on the turbine blades. The faster the blades move, the less the relative impinging speed of the oil and the faster the locomotive moves.

Mechanical transmission is the simplest type; it is mainly used in very low-power switching locomotives and in low-power diesel railcars. Basically it is a clutch and gearbox similar to those used in automobiles. A hydraulic coupling, in some cases, is used in place of a friction clutch.

TYPES OF DIESEL MOTIVE POWER

There are three broad classes of railroad equipment that use diesel engines as prime movers:

1. The light passenger railcar or railbus (up to 200 horsepower), which usually is four-wheeled and has mechanical transmission. It may be designed to haul a light trailer car. Use of such vehicles had become very limited.

2. The four-axle passenger railcar (up to 750 horsepower), which can be operated independently, haul a nonpowered trailer, or be formed into a semipermanent train-set such as a multiple-unit with all or a proportion of the cars powered. In the powered cars the diesel engine and all associated traction equipment, including fuel tanks, are capable of fitting under the floor to free space above the frames for passenger seating. Transmission is either electric or hydraulic. Modern railcars and railcar train-sets are mostly equipped for multiple-unit train operation, with driving control from a single cab.

3. Locomotives (10 to 4,000 horsepower), which may have mechanical transmission if very low-powered or hydraulic transmission for outputs of up to about 2,000 horsepower but in most cases have electric transmission, the choice depending on power output and purpose.

A substantial increase of diesel engine power-to-weight ratios and the application of electronics to component control and diagnostic systems brought significant advances in the efficiency of diesel locomotives in the last quarter of the 20th century. By 1990 a diesel engine with a continuous rating of 3,500 horsepower was available at almost half the weight of a similar model in 1970. At the same time, the fuel efficiency of diesel engines was significantly improved.

Electronics have made a particularly important contribution to the load-hauling capability of diesel-electric locomotives in road freight work by improving adhesion at starting or in grade-climbing. A locomotive accelerating from rest can develop from 33 to 50 percent more tractive force if its powered wheels are allowed to "creep" into a very slight, steady, and finely controlled slip. In a typical "creep control" system, Doppler radar mounted under the locomotive precisely measures true ground speed, against which microprocessors calculate the ideal creep speed limit in the prevailing track conditions and automatically regulate current supply to the traction motors. The process is continuous, so current levels are immediately adjusted to match a change in track parameters. In the 1960s, North Americans considered that a diesel-electric locomotive of 3,000–3,600 horsepower or more must have six motored axles for effective adhesion: two railroads had acquired a small number of eight-motored-axle locomotives, each powered by two diesel engines, with outputs of 5,000–6,600 horsepower. Since the mid-1980s four-axle locomotives of up to 4,000 horsepower have become feasible and are widely employed in fast freight service (though for heavy freight duty six-axle locomotives were still preferred). But today a 4,000-horsepower rating is obtainable from a 16-cylinder diesel engine, whereas in the 1960s a 3,600-horsepower output demanded a 20-cylinder engine. This, coupled with the reduction in the number of locomotives required to haul a given tonnage due to improved adhesion, has been a key factor in decreasing locomotive maintenance costs.

Outside North America, widespread electrification all but ended production of diesel locomotives purpose-built for passenger train haulage in the 1960s. The last development for high-speed diesel service was on British Railways, which, for its nonelectrified trunk routes, mass-produced a semipermanent train-set, the InterCity 125, that had a 2,250-horsepower locomotive at each end of seven or eight intermediate cars. In 1987 one of these sets established a world speed record for diesel traction of 238 km (148 miles) per hour. Some InterCity 125 sets are expected to remain in service under various other designations until well into the 21st century. In North America, Amtrak in the United States and VIA in Canada, as well as some urban mass-transit authorities, still operate diesel locomotives exclusively on passenger trains. Elsewhere road haul diesel locomotives are designed either for exclusive freight haulage or for mixed passenger and freight work.

TRACTION OPERATING METHODS

Multiple-unit connection and operation of locomotives, to adjust power to load and track gradient requirements, is standard practice in North America and is common elsewhere. Where considerable gradients occur or freight trains are unusually long and heavy, concentration of locomotives at a train's head can strain couplings and undesirably delay transmission of full braking power to the train's rearmost cars. In such conditions several railroads, principally in North America, employ crewless "slave" locomotives that are inserted partway down the train. Radio signals transmitted from the train's leading locomotive cause the slave locomotive's controls to respond automatically and correspondingly to all operations of the controls. A world record for freight train weight and length was set in August 1989 on South Africa's electrified, 516-mile (830-km), 3-foot-6-inch (1,065-mm)-gauge Sishen-Saldanha ore line. In the course of research into the feasibility of increasing the line's regular trainloads, a 660-car train grossing 71,600 tons and 4.47 miles (7.2 km) long was run from end to end of the route. Power was furnished by five 5,025-horsepower electric locomotives at the front, four more inserted after the 470th freight car, and at the rear, to avoid overtaxing the traction current supply system, seven 2,900-horsepower diesel locomotives.

After World War II easy directional reversibility of passenger train-sets became increasingly important for intensively operated short- and medium-haul services, to reduce terminal turnaround times and minimize the number of train-sets needed to provide the service. The most popular medium has been the self-powered railcar or multiple-unit train-set, with a driving cab at each end so that reversal requires only that the crew change cabs. An alternative, known as push-pull, has a normal locomotive at one end and, at the other, a nonpowered passenger or baggage car, known as the driving or control trailer, with a driving cab at its extremity. In one direction the locomotive pulls the train; in the other, unmanned, it propels the train, driven via through-train wiring from the control trailer's cab. A potential operating advantage of push-pull as opposed to use of self-powered train-sets on a railroad running both passenger and freight trains is that at night, when passenger operation has ceased, the locomotives can be detached for freight haulage.

TURBINE PROPULSION

In the 1950s gas-turbine instead of diesel propulsion was tried for a few locomotives in the United States and

Britain, but the results did not justify continuing develop-ment. There was a longer but very limited career in rail use for the compact and lightweight gas turbines developed for helicopters that became available in the 1960s. Their power-to-weight ratio, superior to that of contemporary diesel engines, made them preferable for lightweight, high-speed train-sets. They were applied to Canadian-built train-sets placed in service in 1968 between Montreal and Toronto and in 1969 between New York City and Boston, but these were short-lived because of equipment troubles, operating noise, and the cost of fuel. The tech-nology has not been entirely abandoned, however. At the end of the 20th and beginning of the 21st centuries, the Bombardier company of Canada presented its gas-turbine JetTrain locomotive as an alternative to electric traction for new North American high-speed systems.

Several attempts were made to adapt the steam tur-bine to railroad traction. One of the first such experiments was a Swedish locomotive built in 1921. Other proto-types followed in Europe and the United States. They all functioned, but they made their appearance too late to compete against the diesel and electrification.

A fter the first crude beginnings, railroad-car design took divergent courses in North America and Europe, because of differing economic conditions and technological developments. Early cars on both continents were largely of two-axle design, but passenger-car builders soon began constructing cars with three and then four axles, the latter arranged in two four-wheel swivel trucks, or bogies. The trucks resulted in smoother riding qualities and also spread the weight of heavy vehicles over more axles.

FREIGHT CARS

Throughout the world the great majority of freight cars for all rail gauges are built with four axles, divided between two trucks. Because of the layout constraints of some freight terminals, several European railroads still purchase a proportion of two-axle vehicles, but even these have a much longer wheelbase and hence a considerably larger load capacity than similar cars in the past. Some bulk mineral cars in Germany and the United States have been built with two three-axle trucks, and Russia and various other former Soviet states still have a number of freight cars carried on four two-axle trucks; these are the world's largest. Concern to maximize payload capacity in relation to tare vehicle weight has led to U.S. and European adoption of articulation for cars in certain uses, notably intermodal transport. In this system a car comprises several frames or bodies (usually not more than five), which, where they adjoin, are permanently coupled and mounted on a single truck.

One type of vehicle that is virtually extinct is the caboose, or brake-van. With modern air-braking systems, the security of a very long train can be assured by fixing to its end car's brake pipe a telemetry device that continually monitors pressure and automatically transmits its findings to the locomotive cab.

Before World War II, freight cars consisted almost entirely of four basic types: the semiwalled open car, the fully covered boxcar, the flatcar, and the tank car. Since then, railroads and car builders have developed a wide range of car types designed specifically for the ideal handling and competitive transport of individual goods or commodities. At the same time, the payload weight of bulk commodities that can be conveyed in a single car without undue track wear has been significantly increased by advances in truck design and, in North America, by growing use of aluminum instead of steel for bodywork, to reduce the car's own tare weight. In Europe and North America, where highway competition demands faster rail movement of time-sensitive freight, cars for such traffic as perishable goods, high-value merchandise, and containers are designed to run at 75 miles (120 km) per hour. The French and German railways both operate some selected merchandise and intermodal trains at up to 100 miles (160 km) per hour to achieve overnight delivery between centres up to about 600 miles (1,000 km) apart. In the United States, container trains travelling at 75 miles (120 km) per hour where route characteristics allow are scheduled to cover 2,200 miles (about 3,500 km) in 52 hours.

In Europe and North America open cars for bulk mineral transport are generally designed for rapid discharge, either by being bodily rotated or through power-operated doors in the floor or lower sides of their hopper bodies. Modern North American four-axle coal cars typically have 100–110 tons' payload capacity. In Europe, where tighter clearances necessitate smaller body dimensions and track is not designed for axle loadings as high as those accepted in North America, the payload capacity of similar four-axle cars is between 60 and 65 tons. High-sided open cars also are built with fully retractable sliding roofs, either metal or canvas, to facilitate overhead loading and discharge of cargoes needing protection in transit. In a variant of this concept for the transport of steel coil in particular, the sidewalls and roof are in two or more separate, integral, and overlapping assemblies; these can be slid over or under each other for loading or discharge of one section of the vehicle without exposing the remainder of the load.

Fully covered hopper cars or tank cars are available with pressure discharge for bulk movement of a variety of powders and solids. Tank cars are also purpose-designed for safe transport of a wide range of hazardous fluids.

Because of the rapid growth of intermodal transport in North America, boxcar design has seen fewer changes there than in western Europe. For ease of mechanized loading of palletized freight, modern European boxcars are built with their entire sidewalls divided into sliding and overlapping doors. Another option is to replace the sidewalls with a fully retractable, material-covered framework so that the interior of the vehicle can be wholly opened up for loading or discharge. A typical North American boxcar for bulky but comparatively light cargo may have a load-area volume of up to 10,000 cubic feet (283 cubic metres); that of a modern four-axle European boxcar is 5,700 cubic feet (161.4 cubic metres). Boxcars are often fitted internally with movable partitions or other special fittings to brace loads such as products in sacks. Vehicles for transport of fragile merchandise have cushioned draft gear that absorbs any shocks sustained by the cars in train or yard shunting movement.

The automobile industry's concentration of manufacture of individual models at specific plants has increased the railroads' share of its transportation. As distances from manufacturing plant to dealer increase—and in many cases these involve international transits—the security and economy offered by the railroad as a bulk transporter of finished autos have become more appreciated. In North America vertical clearances allow automobiles to be carried in triple-deck freight cars, but in Europe the limit is double-deck. Retractable flaps enable each deck of adjoining cars to be connected to form drive-through roadways on both levels for loading and discharge of an auto-transporter train. Such cars also are used for a type of service for motorists that is widespread in Europe but confined to one route in the United States: trains that combine transporters for autos with passenger cars for their occupants. These are mostly operated between ports or inland cities and vacation areas in the peak season. Special-purpose cars also have been developed for inter-plant movement of automobile components, including engines and body assemblies, and for regular delivery of spare parts to distribution areas.

PASSENGER CARS

The first passenger cars were simply road coaches with flanged wheels. Almost from the beginning, railroads in the United States began to use longer, eight-wheel cars riding on two four-wheel trucks. In Britain and Europe, however, cars with more than six wheels were not introduced until the 1870s. Modern cars, for both local and long-distance service, have an entrance at one or both ends of the car.

An illustrative woodcut of the first steam railroad passenger train in America.
Library of Congress Prints and Photographs Division

Commuter-service cars also have additional centre doors. Flexible connections between cars give passengers access to any car of a moving train, except when the coupling together of self-powered, reversible train-sets for multiple-unit operation makes passenger communication between one train-set and another impossible, because there is a driving cab at the extremity of each unit.

In the United States modern passenger cars are usually 85 feet (25 metres) long. In continental Europe the standard length of cars for conventional locomotive-hauled main-line service is now about 87 feet (26 metres), but the cars of some high-speed train-sets are shorter, as are those of many urban transport multiple-unit cars and of railcars for secondary local services. Modern British cars are 64.5 or 75 feet (roughly 19.5 or 22.5 metres) in length. The sharper curves of narrow-gauge railroads generally demand shorter length.

Reduction of the weight of a car's mechanical structures has become important to minimize the energy consumed in traction, particularly for high-speed vehicles. Car bodies are still mostly of steel, but use of aluminum is increasing, especially for passenger cars and for high-speed train cars. Modular construction techniques, simplifying the adaptation of a car body to different interior layouts and furniture, has encouraged railroads to standardize basic car structures for a variety of service requirements. For this reason, construction of small numbers of special-purpose cars demanding nonstandard bodies is not favoured; an example is the dome observation car, with a raised, glass roof section, popular in North America.

Modern truck design is the product of lengthy research into the interaction of wheel and rail, and into suspension systems, with the dual objectives of stable ride quality and minimum wear of track and wheel sets, especially at very high speed. The trucks of many modern cars have air suspension or a combination of air and metal springing. The entrance doors of all modern European cars are power-operated and capable of interlocking from a central control by the train's conductor to prevent improper passenger use when the train is moving. Efficient soundproofing and insulation of car interiors from external noise and undesirable climatic conditions have become a major concern, particularly because of more widespread air-conditioning of cars. Very-high-speed train-sets must have their entire interior, including intercar gangways, externally sealed to prevent passenger discomfort from air pressure changes when they thread tunnels.

BRAKE SYSTEMS

There are two principal types of continuous train braking system: vacuum, which now survives mostly on railroads in the developing world, and compressed air, the inherently greater efficiency of which has been improved by modern electric or electronic control systems. With either system brake application in the train's driving cab is transmitted to all its vehicles; if a train becomes uncoupled on the move, interruption of the through-train connection of controls automatically applies brakes to both parts of the train. Modern passenger cars—and some freight cars—have disc brakes instead of wheel-tread shoes. Wheel sets of cars operating at 100 miles (160 km) per hour or more are fitted with devices to prevent wheel slip under heavy braking. On European cars designed for operation at 125 miles (200 km) per hour or more, and on Japanese Shinkansen train-sets, disc braking of wheel sets is supplemented by fitting electromagnetic track brakes to car trucks. Activated at the start of deceleration from high speed, these retard by the frictional resistance generated when bar magnets are lowered into contact with the rails. Some Shinkansen train-sets have been fitted with eddy current instead of electromagnetic track brakes. The eddy-current brake makes no contact with the rail (so is not subject to frictional wear) and is more powerful, but it sets up strong electromagnetic fields that require reinforced immunization of signaling circuitry. Also, where operation of trains so equipped is intensive, there is a risk that eddy-current braking might heat rails to a degree that could cause them to deform.

AUTOMATIC BODY TILTING

The permissible maximum speed of a passenger train through curves is the level beyond which a railroad considers passengers will suffer unacceptable centrifugal force; the limit beyond which derailment becomes a risk is considerably higher. On a line built for exclusive use of high-speed trains, curved track can be canted, or superelevated, to a degree specifically suited to those trains. The cant can be steeper than on a mixed-traffic route, where it must be a compromise between the ideal for fast passenger and slow, heavy freight trains, to avoid the latter bearing too severely on the curve's inner rail. Consequently, on a dedicated high-speed passenger line, the extra degree of superelevation can raise quite significantly the curving speed possible without discomforting passengers from the effects of centrifugal force.

On existing mixed-traffic lines, however, passenger train speed through curves can be increased by equipping cars with devices that automatically tilt car bodies up to 9° toward the inward side of the curve, thereby adding to the degree of cant imparted by the track's superelevation. There are two types of automatic body-tilting system. A passive system is more complex. It reacts to track curvature: that is, the body-tilting mechanism responds retroactively, if only by a fraction of a second, to its gauging of deficiency in the track's superelevation relative to the speed at which the vehicle is traveling. An active system employs sensors to detect the transition to curved track and controls to measure the progressive degree of tilt applied by the tilt-operating mechanism in response to the sensor's electronic signals as the curve itself is threaded. The sensors are usually fitted to the front vehicle of a tilt-body train-set so that the tilt-body equipment on following vehicles operates in smooth, split-second anticipation of a track curve's development. An active system can apply a higher degree of body-tilt than a passive system, but active systems impose constraints on some aspects of car design and add to the car's capital and maintenance costs.

CARS FOR DAYTIME SERVICE

The preferred interior layout of seating cars throughout the world is the open saloon (or parlor car), with the seats in bays on either side of a central aisle. This arrangement maximizes passenger capacity per car. Density of seating is less in an intercity car than in a short-haul commuter service car; the cars of some heavily used urban rapid-transit railroads, such as those of Japanese cities and Hong Kong, have minimal seating to maximize stand-ing room. European cars of segregated six- or eight-seat compartments served by a corridor on one side of the car survive in considerable numbers. Marketing concern to tailor accommodation to the needs of specific passenger groups, such as businesspeople and families, has led to German production of some cars combining saloon and compartment sections and to French semi-compartment enclosure of the seating bays on one side of the first-class cars in TGV train-sets.

The great majority of cars in short-haul commuter ser-vice are still single-deck, but to maximize seating capacity there is an increasing use of double-deck cars for such oper-ations in North America, Europe, and Australia. North American operators have tended to prefer a design that limits the upper level to a gallery along each side wall, but in most double-deck cars the upper level is wholly floor-separated from the lower. A four-car, double-deck electric multiple-unit of the Paris commuter network in France is 324 feet (98 metres) long and can seat 534 passengers.

Double-deck cars, suitably furnished, are found in long-haul intercity operation by Amtrak in the United States and in some Japanese Shinkansen train-sets. Since 1996 French National Railways has operated TGV "Duplex" train-sets with every car double-decked

A double-deck passenger train departure. Shutterstock.com

except for the locomotives at each end. These cars exemplify modern weight-saving construction. French National Railways insists on a static load limit of 37,000 pounds (17,000 kg) on any axle of a vehicle travelling its high-speed lines. The French also prefer to articulate adjoining, nonpowered cars of their TGV train-sets over a single two-axle truck. Consequently, each double-deck car, roughly 65 feet (20 metres) long and providing up to 96 comfortable seats, must weigh no more than 74,000 pounds (34,000 kg).

Because of its high operating costs, particularly in terms of staff, dining or restaurant car service of main meals entirely prepared and cooked in an on-train kitchen has been greatly reduced since World War II. Full meal service is widely available on intercity trains, but many railroads have switched to airline methods of wholly or partly preparing dishes in depots on the ground and finishing them for service in on-train galleys or small-size kitchens. This change is sometimes accompanied by sub-stitution of at-seat service in place of a dining car, which has lost favour because its seats earn no fare revenue. At the same time, there has been a considerable increase in buffet counters for service of light snacks and drinks and also through-train trolley service of light refreshments. Most European railroads franchise their on-train cater-ing services to specialist companies.

CARS FOR OVERNIGHT TRAVEL

A crude car with bedding provision was operated in the United States as early as 1837, but sleeping cars with enclosed bedrooms did not appear until the last quarter of the 19th century. The compartments of most modern sleeping cars have, against one wall only, normal seat-ing that is convertible to one bed; one or two additional beds are on hinged bases that are folded into the opposite compartment wall when not in use. A low-priced version of this concept is popular in Europe, where it is known as "couchette"; the compartments are devoid of washbasins so that convertible seating and beds can be installed on both walls, and the beds do not have innerspring (sprung) mattresses. Double-deck sleeping cars operated by Amtrak in the United States have on their upper floor "economy" rooms for single or double occupancy; on the lower floor are similar rooms, a family room, a room specially arranged for handicapped travelers, and shower rooms. Rooms in modern European cars are of common size, the price of use depending on the number of beds to be occupied.

INTERMODAL VEHICLES

An important competitive development has been the perfection of intermodal freight transport systems, in

THE PULLMAN CAR

The first car designed for comfortable nighttime travel was the Pullman sleeper, which was commercially introduced by American industrialist George M. Pullman and his friend Ben Field in 1865. Pullman was born on March 3, 1831, in Brocton, N.Y. He moved to Chicago in 1855, accumulated some capital as a contractor, and began to devise a sleeping car. The first real Pullman car was the 1865 "Pioneer," invented jointly with Field. It contained folding upper berths and seat cushions that could be extended to make lower berths. Pullman became president of the Pullman Palace Car Company, organized in 1867, which built sleeping cars and operated them under contract to the railroads.

To house his employees, Pullman built the town of Pullman, located just south of Chicago (and later incorporated into it). The town (much of which is still standing) includes both public buildings, such as the impressive Victorian-style Hotel Florence and a greenstone church, and private dwellings. The paternalistic company-owned town was a widely discussed social experiment; a strike there by Pullman employees in 1894 led to sympathy strikes across the United States and a call for Pullman cars to be boycotted. Pullman died in Chicago on Oct. 19, 1897.

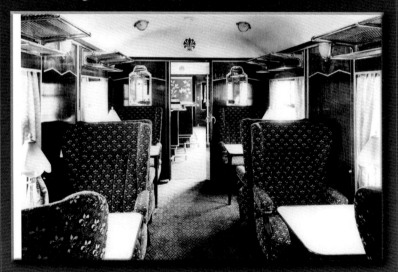

The Pullman car Pegasus Bar. SSPL via Getty Images

which highway truck trailers or marine shipping containers are set on railroad flatcars. In North America and Europe they have been the outstanding growth area of rail freight activity since World War II. For the largest U.S. railroads, only coal now generates more carloadings per annum than intermodal traffic.

In overload intermodal transport the economy of the railroad as a bulk long-distance hauler is married to the superior efficiency and flexibility of highway transport for shorter-distance collection and delivery of individual consignments. Intermodal transportation also makes use of rail for the long haul accessible and viable to a manufacturer that is not directly rail-served and has no private siding.

DEVELOPMENT

Initially, the emphasis in North America was on the rail piggybacking of highway trailers on flatcars (TOFC), which the Southern Pacific Railroad pioneered in 1953. By 1958 the practice had been adopted by 42 railroads; and by the beginning of the 1980s U.S. railroads were recording more than two million piggyback carloadings a year. In Europe, few railroads had clearances ample enough to accept a highway box trailer piggybacked on a flatcar of normal frame height. As shipping lines developed their container transport business in the early 1960s, European railroads concentrated initially on container-on-flatcar (COFC) intermodal systems. A few offered a range of small containers of their own design for internal traffic, but until the 1980s domestic as well as deep-sea COFC in Europe was dominated by the standard sizes of maritime containers. In the 1980s an increasing proportion of Europe's internal COFC traffic used the swapbody, or demountable, which is similar in principle to, but more lightly constructed, cheaper, and easier to transship than, the maritime container; the latter has to withstand stacking several deep on board ship and at ports, which is not a requisite for the swapbody. As its name suggests, the swapbody has highway truck or trailer body characteristics.

The container took on a growing role in North American intermodal transportation in the 1980s. American President Intermodal decided that containers originating from Pacific Rim countries to destinations in the Midwest and eastern United States were better sent by rail from western seaboard ports than shipped through the Panama Canal. To optimize the economics of rail landbridging, the shipping line furthered development of lightweight railcars articulating five low-slung well frames on each of which containers could be double-stacked within, or with minimal modification of, the vertical clearances of the principal route between West Coast ports and Chicago. At the same time, the shipping line marketed containers off-loaded in the east as the medium for rail shipment of merchandise from the east to the western states. This was influential in stimulating new interest in the container as a medium for domestic door-to-door transportation. Other shipping lines copied American President's lead; railroads enlarged clearances to extend the scope of double-stack container transportation to the eastern and southern seaboards (Canadian railroads followed suit); and in the later 1980s both double-stack operation and the container's share of total North American intermodal traffic rapidly expanded.

OPERATIONS

The overhead costs of COFC and TOFC are considerable. Both require terminals with high-capacity transshipment cranage and considerable space for internal traffic movement and storage. TOFC also has a cost penalty in the deadweight of the highway trailers' running gear that has to be included in a TOFC train's payload. Two principal courses have been taken by railroads to improve the economics of their intermodal operations. One is to limit their transshipment terminals to strategically located and well-equipped hubs, from which highway collection and delivery services radiate over longer distances; as a result, the railroad can carry the greater part of its intermodal traffic in full terminal-to-terminal trainloads, or unit trains. The other course has been to minimize the tare weight of rail intermodal vehicles by such techniques as skeletal frame construction and, as in the double-stack COFC units described above, articulation of car frames over a single truck. Even so, North American railroads have not been able to make competitively priced TOFC remunerative unless the rail component of the transit is more than about 600 miles (1,000 km).

Two different managerial approaches to intermodal freight service have developed in the United States. Some of the major railroads have organized to manage and market complete door-to-door transits themselves; others prefer simply to wholesale intermodal train space to third parties. These third parties organize, manage, and bill the whole door-to-door transit for an individual consignor.

Given the shorter intercity distances, European railroads have found it more difficult to operate viable TOFC services. The loading of a highway box trailer on a railcar of normal frame height without infringing European railroads' reduced vertical clearances was solved by French National Railways in the 1950s. The answer was a railcar with floor pockets into which the trailer's wheels could be slotted so that the trailer's floor ended up parallel with that of the railcar. Even so, there were limitations on the acceptable height of box trailers. Other railroads were prompted to begin TOFC in the 1960s when the availability of heavy tonnage cranes at new container terminals simplified the placing of trailers in the so-called "pocket" cars. Initial TOFC service development was primarily over long and mostly international trade routes, such as from the Netherlands, Belgium, and northern Germany to southern Germany, Austria, and Italy.

The Germans, followed by the Austrians and Swiss and then other European countries, developed a particularly costly intermodal technology called "Rolling Highway" (Rollende Landstrasse), because it employs low-floor cars that, coupled into a train, form an uninterrupted drive-on, drive-off roadway for highway trucks or tractor-trailer rigs. Rolling Highway cars are carried on four- or six-axle trucks with wheels of only 14-inch (36-cm) diameter so as to lower their floors sufficiently to secure the extra vertical clearance for highway vehicles loaded without their wheels pocketed. Platforms bridge the gap between the close-coupled railcars. To allow highway vehicles to drive on or off the train yet enable a locomotive to couple to it without difficulty, the train-end low-floor cars have normal-height draft-gear headstocks that are hinged and can be swung aside to open up the train's roadway. Truck drivers travel in a passenger car added to the train.

In the face of growing trade between northwestern and southeastern Europe, Austria and Switzerland have imposed restraints on use of their countries as a transit corridor by over-the-highway freight to safeguard their environments. Primarily to provide for increase in intermodal traffic, and in particular Rolling Highway trains, the Swiss parliament approved plans to bore new rail tunnels on each of its key north-south transalpine routes, the Gotthard and the Lötschen. The Lötschberg Base Tunnel, the world's longest overland tunnel—a 21.5-mile (34.6-km) rail link—took eight years to build, and when full rail service began in 2007, it slashed the train journey between Germany and Italy from 3.5 hours to less than 2 hours. The 35-mile (57-km) Gotthard Base Tunnel—an even more ambitious project—is scheduled for completion by 2017. Both tunnels will be much longer than older tunnels located higher up in the passes; thus their tracks will be free of the present routes' steep gradients and sharp curves on either side of their tunnels.

PASSENGER INTERMODALS

To save motorists the negotiation of mountain passes, especially in winter, two Swiss railroads shuttle drive-on, drive-off trains for automobiles between terminals at the extremities of their transalpine tunnels. This practice has been elaborated for Channel Tunnel rail transport of private automobiles, buses, and trucks between Britain and France. The tunnel's rail traffic is partly conventional trains, but it has been bored to dimensions that allow auto transporter trains to employ cars of unprecedented size. Consequently, these trains are limited to shuttle operation between terminals on the British and French coasts. The fully enclosed, double-deck cars for automobile traffic measure 18 feet 4 inches (5.5 metres) high and 13 feet 5 inches (4 metres) wide; the latter dimension allows room for automobile passengers, who are carried in their vehicle, to dismount and use the car's toilet or auto-buffet while the train threads the tunnel. The transporter cars for buses and trucks are single-deck.

I deally, a railroad should be built in a straight line, over level ground, between large centres of trade and travel. In practice, this ideal is rarely approached. The location engineer, faced with the terrain to be traversed, must balance the cost of construction against annual maintenance and operating costs, as well as against the probable traffic volume and profit.

LOCATION AND CONSTRUCTION

In areas of dense population and heavy industrial activities, the railroads were generally built for heavy duty, with minimum grades and curvature, heavy bridges, and perhaps multiple tracks. Examples include most of the main-line railroads of Britain and the European continent. In North and South America and elsewhere the country was sparsely settled, and the railroads had to be built at minimal costs. Thus, the lines were of lighter construction, with sharper grades and curves. As traffic grew, main routes were improved to increase their capacity and to reduce operating costs.

The gauge, or distance between the inside faces of the running rails, can affect the cost of building and equipping a railroad. About 60 percent of the world's railroad mileage has been built to standard gauge, 4 feet 8.5 inches (1,435 mm). However, a considerable mileage of lines with narrower gauges has been constructed, mainly in undeveloped and sparsely settled countries. Use of a narrow gauge permits some saving in space. In addition, narrow-gauge cars and locomotives are generally smaller, lighter, and less costly than those used on standard-gauge lines. Disadvantages of a narrow gauge include the limitation on speed because of reduced lateral stability and limitations on the size of locomotives and cars.

The advent of modern high-capacity earth-moving machinery, developed mainly for highway construction, has made it economically feasible for many railroads to eliminate former adverse grades and curves through line changes. Graders, bulldozers, and similar equipment make it possible to dig deeper cuts through hillsides and to make higher fills where necessary to smooth out the profile of the track. Modern equipment has also helped to improve railroad roadbeds in other ways. Where the roadbed is unstable, for example, injecting concrete grout into the subgrade under pressure is a widely used technique. In planning roadbed improvements, as well as in new construction, railroads have drawn on modern soil-engineering techniques.

When track is laid on a completed roadbed, its foundation is ballast, usually of crushed rock, slag, or volcanic ash. The sleepers, or crossties, to which the rails are fastened, are embedded in the ballast. This is tightly compacted or tamped around the sleepers to keep the track precisely leveled and aligned. Efficient drainage of the ballast is critically important to prevent its destabilization. The depth of ballast depends on the characteristics of a line's traffic; it must be considerably greater on a track carrying frequent high-speed passenger trains, for example, than on one used by medium-speed commuter trains. As an example of the parameters adopted for construction of a new high-speed line in Europe, in Germany the total width of a roadbed to carry two standard-gauge tracks averages about 45 feet (13.5 metres). The tracks are laid so

Crushed rock is used as ballast for railroad track to give it support.
Shutterstock.com

that their centres are 15 feet 5 inches (4.7 metres) apart. The standard depth of ballast is 12 inches (30 cm), but it is packed to a depth of 20 inches (50 cm) around the ends of the crossties or sleepers to ensure lateral stability.

In some situations where track maintenance is difficult, such as in some tunnels, or where drainage problems are acute, ballast and sleepers are replaced by continuous reinforced concrete support of the rails. This system, known as slab track, maintains accurate track geometry without maintenance attention for much longer periods than ballasted track, but its reduced maintenance costs are offset by higher first and renewal costs.

In Europe and Asia considerable stretches of high-speed railroad have been and are being built alongside multilane intercity highways. This simplifies location of the new railroad and minimizes its intrusion in rural landscape. Such sharing of alignment is feasible because tracks for the dedicated use of modern high-speed train-sets can be built with curves and gradients not far short of the most severe parameters tolerated in contemporary express highway construction.

RAIL

The modern railroad rail has a flat bottom, and its cross section is much like an inverted T. An English engineer, Charles Vignoles, is credited with the invention of this design in the 1830s. A similar design also was developed by Robert L. Stevens, president of the Camden and Amboy Railroad in the United States.

Present-day rail is, in appearance, very similar to the early designs of Vignoles and Stevens. Actually, however, it is a highly refined product in terms of both engineering and metallurgy. Much study and research have produced designs that minimize internal stresses under the weight of traffic and thus prolong rail life. Sometimes the rail surface is hardened to reduce the wear of the rail under extremely heavy cars or on sharp curves. After they have been rolled at the steel mills, rails are allowed to cool slowly in special boxes. This controlled cooling minimizes internal shatter cracks, which at one time were a major cause of broken rails in track.

In Europe a standard rail length of 98 feet 5 inches (30 metres) is common. The weight of rail, for principal main-line use, is from about 110 pounds per yard (about 55 kg per metre) to 130 pounds per yard (65 kg per metre).

Railroads in the United States and Canada have used T-rails of hundreds of different cross sections. Many of these different sections are still in use, but there is a strong trend to standardizing on a few sections. Most new rail in North America weighs 115 or 132 pounds per yard (57.5 or 66 kg per metre). The standard American rail section has

A present-day train waiting at a station. Shutterstock.com

a length of 39 feet (12 metres). Some ore mining railroads in Western Australia employ rail weighing about 68 kg per metre (about 136 pounds per yard).

One of the most important developments is the welding of standard rails into long lengths. This continuous welded rail results in a smoother track that requires less maintenance. In North America the rail is usually welded into lengths of between 320 yards and one-quarter mile (290 and 400 metres). Once laid in track, these quarter-mile lengths are often welded together in turn to form rails several miles long without a break.

Welded rail was tried for the first time in 1933 in the United States. It was not until the 1950s, however, that railroads turned to welded rail in earnest. Welded rail is now standard practice, or extensively used, on railroads throughout the industrialized world and is being adopted elsewhere to the extent that railroads' finances allow.

Controlling the temperature expansion of long welded rails has proved not so difficult as first thought. It has been found that the problem can be minimized by extensive anchorage of the rails to the sleepers or ties to prevent them from moving when the temperature changes, by the use of a heavy ballast section, and by heating the rails before laying to a temperature close to the mean temperature prevailing in the particular locality.

RAIL FITTINGS

Whether in standard or long welded lengths, rails are joined to each other and kept in alignment by fishplates or joint bars. The offset-head spike is the least expensive way of fastening the rails to wooden crossties, but several different types of screw spikes and clips are used. The rails may be attached directly to wooden crossties, but except on minor lines it is standard practice to seat the rail in a tie plate that distributes the load over a wider area of the tie. A screw or clip fitting must be used to attach rails to concrete ties. A pad of rubber or other resilient material is always used between the rail and a concrete tie.

SLEEPERS (CROSSTIES)

Timber has been used for railroad sleepers or ties almost from the beginning, and it is still the most common material for this purpose. The modern wood sleeper is treated with preservative chemical to improve its life. The cost of wood ties has risen steadily, creating interest in ties of other materials.

Steel ties have been used in certain European, African, and Asian countries. Concrete ties, usually reinforced with steel rods or wires, or ties consisting of concrete blocks joined by steel spacing bars are the popular alternative to wooden ties. A combination of concrete ties and long welded rails produces an exceptionally solid and smooth-riding form of track. Concrete ties have been standardized for the main lines of most European railroads and in Japan. Use of concrete elsewhere is increasing—although in North America, which has no European- or Asian-style high-speed rail and where hardwood for traditional cross-ties is cheap, there is no widespread use.

TRACK MAINTENANCE

Modern machinery enables a small group of workers to maintain a relatively long stretch of railroad track. Machines are available to do all the necessary track maintenance tasks: removing and inserting ties, tamping the ballast, cleaning the ballast, excavation and replacement of worn ballast, spiking rail, tightening bolts, and aligning the track. Some machines are equipped to perform more than one task—for example, ballast tamping combined with track lining and leveling. Mechanized equipment also can renew rail, either in conventional bolted lengths or with long welded lengths; a modern machine of this type has built-in devices to lift and pass the old rail to flatcars at its rear and to bring forward and deposit new rail, so it dispenses with separate crane vehicles.

Complete sections of track—rails and crossties—may be prefabricated and laid in the track by mechanical means. Rail-grinding machines run over the track to even out irregularities in the rail surface. Track-measurement cars, under their own power or coupled into regular trains, can record all aspects of track alignment and riding quality on moving charts so that maintenance forces can pinpoint the specific locations needing corrective work. Detector cars move over the main-line tracks at intervals with electronic-inspection apparatus to locate any internal flaws in the rails.

The mechanization of track maintenance after World War II has constituted a technologic revolution comparable to the development of the diesel locomotive and electrification. Precision of operation, especially in maintenance of true track alignment, has gained much from the application of electronics to the machines' measuring and control devices. In Europe in particular, highly sophisticated maintenance machines have come into use.

OPERATIONS AND CONTROL

Because a railroad's "factory"—its plant and train operations—may be spread out over thousands of miles and hundreds of communities, and because its trains use fixed tracks, unlike automobiles or airplanes, it has operating and service problems in some respects more complex than those of a major manufacturing installation. It is not surprising, therefore, that railroads have been among the pioneers in the use of improved methods of communication and control, from the telegraph to the computer and automation techniques.

COMMUNICATIONS

Railroads were among the first to adopt the electric telegraph and the telephone, both for dispatching trains and for handling other business messages. Today, the railroads are among the larger operators of electronic communications systems.

RADIO

Railroads began experimenting with radio at a very early date, but it became practical to use train radio on a large scale only after World War II, when compact and reliable very-high-frequency two-way equipment was developed.

In train operations radio permits communication between the front and rear of a long train, between two trains, and between trains and ground traffic controllers. It also is the medium for automatic transmission to ground staff of data generated by the microprocessor-based diagnostic equipment of modern traction and train-sets.

In terminals two-way radio greatly speeds yard-switching work. Through its use, widely separated elements of mechanized track-maintenance gangs can maintain contact with each other and with oncoming trains. Supervisory personnel often use radio in automobiles to maintain contact with the operations under their control.

As the demand for more railroad communication lines has grown, the traditional lineside telegraph wire system has been superseded. As early as 1959, the Pacific Great Eastern Railway in western Canada began to use microwave radio for all communications, doing away almost entirely with line wires. Other railroads all over the world turned to microwave in the 1970s and '80s. More recently many railroads have adopted optical-fibre transmission systems. The high-capacity optical-fibre cable, lightweight and immune to electromagnetic interference, can integrate voice, data, and video channels in one system.

COMPUTERS

A major reason for the growing use of microwave and optical-fibre systems is the tremendously increased demand for circuits that have developed from the railroads' widespread use of electronic computers.

Earlier, railroads had been among the leaders in adopting punched-card and other advanced techniques of data processing. In the 1970s and '80s there was a strong trend toward "total information" systems built around the computer. In rail freight operation, each field reporting point, usually a freight-yard office or terminal, is equipped with a computer input device. Through this device, full information about every car movement (or other action) taking place at that point can be placed directly into the central computer, usually located at company headquarters. From data received from all the field reporting points on the railroad, the computer can be programmed to produce a variety of outputs. These include train-consist reports (listing cars) for the terminal next ahead of a train, car-location reports for the railroad's customer-service offices, car-movement information for the car-records department, revenue information for the accounting department, plus traffic-flow data and commodity statistics useful in market research and data on the freight car needs at each location to aid in distributing empty cars for loading. Tracing of individual car movements can be elaborated by adoption of automatic car identification systems, in which each vehicle is fitted with an individually coded transponder that is read by strategically located electronic scanners at trackside. Major customers can be equipped for direct access to the railroad computer system so that they can instantly monitor the status of their freight consignments. Relation of real-time inputs to non-variable data banked in computer memory enables the railroad's central computer to generate customer invoices automatically. Data banks can be developed to identify the optimal routing and equipment required for specific freight between given terminals so that price quotations for new business can be swiftly computer-generated.

Computers and microprocessors have found many other uses as a railroad management aid. For example, daily data on each locomotive's mileage and any special attention it has needed can be fed by its operating depot into a central computer banking historical data on every locomotive operated by the railroad. In the past, many railroads scheduled locomotive overhauls at arbitrarily

assessed intervals, but use of a computer base enables over-
haul of an individual locomotive to be precisely related to
need so that it is not unnecessarily withdrawn from traffic. The same procedure can be applied to passenger cars.
Systems have been developed that optimize economical
use of locomotives by integrated analysis of traffic trends,
the real-time location of locomotives, and the railroad's
route characteristics to generate the ideal assignment of
each locomotive from day to day.

Computerization has given a railroad's managers a
complete, up-to-the-minute picture of almost every phase
of its operations. Such complete information and control
systems have proved a powerful tool for optimizing railroad operations, controlling costs, and producing better
service.

SIGNALING

Railroad signals are a form of communication designed to
inform the train crew, particularly the engine crew, of track
conditions ahead and to tell it how to operate the train.

Methods of controlling train operations evolved over
many years of trial and error. A common method in the
early years was to run trains on a time-interval system; i.e.,
a train was required to leave a station a certain number of
minutes behind an earlier train moving in the same direction. The development of distance-interval systems was
a great improvement. In these so-called block systems, a
train is prevented from entering a specific section of track
until the train already in that section has left it.

Operation of single-track routes on the basis of a
timetable alone, which was common on early lines in the
United States, had the disadvantage that, if one train were
delayed, others also would be delayed, since it was impossible to change the meeting points. By using the telegraph,

and later the telephone, the dispatcher could issue orders to keep trains moving in unusual circumstances or to operate extra trains as required. This "timetable–train order" system is still used on many lines in the United States and Canada as well as in developing countries. It is often supplemented with automatic block signals to provide an additional safety factor, and radio is increasingly the means of communication between dispatchers and train crews.

TYPES OF SIGNALS

The earliest form of railroad signal was simply a flag by day or a lamp at night. The first movable signal was a revolving board, introduced in the 1830s, followed in 1841 by the semaphore signal. One early type of American signal consisted of a large ball that was hoisted to the top of a pole to inform the engineman that he might proceed (hence, the origin of the term *highball*).

The semaphore signal was nearly universal until the early years of the 20th century, when it began to be superseded by the colour-light signal, which uses powerful electric lights to display its aspects. These are usually red, green, and yellow, either singly or in simultaneous display of two colours. The different colours are obtained either by rotating appropriate roundels or colour filters in front of a single beam or by providing separate bulbs and lenses for each colour. The number of lights and the range of aspects available from one signal can vary depending on its purpose. For instance, additional lights may be installed to the left or right of the main lights to warn a driver of divergence ahead from the through track. In Britain suitably angled strips of white lights are added to signals and illuminated when a divergent track is signaled. Red (stop or danger), green (track clear), and yellow (warning) have the same basic significance worldwide, but

A colour-light signal indicating how the train can proceed. Eliot Elisofon/
Time & Life Pictures/Getty Images

in Europe particularly they also are used in combinations of two colours to convey meanings that can vary from one railroad to another. Colour-light signaling is now standard on all but some minor rural lines of the world's principal railways, and its use is spreading elsewhere.

AUTOMATED SYSTEMS

The basis of much of today's railroad signaling is the automatic block system, introduced in 1872 and one of the first examples of automation. It uses track circuits that are short-circuited by the wheels and axles of a train, putting the signals to the rear of the train, and to the front as well on single track, at the danger aspect. A track circuit is made by the two rails of a section of track, insulated at their ends. Electric current, fed into the section at one end, flows through a relay at the opposite end. The wheels of the train will then short-circuit the current supply and de-energize the relay.

In a conventional automatic block system, permissible headway between trains is determined by the fixed length of each block system and is therefore invariable. Modern electronics has made possible a so-called "moving block" system, in which block length is determined not by fixed ground distance but by the relative speeds and distance from each other of successive trains. In a typical moving block system, track devices transmit to receivers on each train continuous coded data on the status of trains ahead. Apparatus on a train compares this data with the train's own location and speed, projects a safe stopping distance ahead, and continuously calculates maximum speed for maintenance of that headway. Moving block has been devised essentially for urban rapid-transit rail systems with heavy peak-hour traffic and on which maximum train speeds are not high; in such applications its flexibility by comparison with fixed block increases the possible throughput of trains over one track in a given period of time.

To ensure observance of restrictive signals, a basic form of automatic train control has been used by many major railroads since the 1920s. When a signal aspect is restrictive, an electromagnetic device is activated between the rails, which in turn causes an audible warning to sound in the cab of any train passing over it. If the operator fails to respond appropriately, after a short interval the train brakes are applied automatically. A refinement, generally known as automatic train protection (ATP), has been developed since World War II to provide continuous control of train speed. It has been applied principally to busy urban commuter and rapid-transit routes and to European and Japanese intercity high-speed routes. A display in the cab reproduces either the aspects of signals ahead or up to 10 different instructions of speed to be maintained, decelerated to, or accelerated to, according to the state of the track ahead. Failure to respond to a restrictive instruction automatically initiates both power reduction and braking. The cab displays are activated by on-train processing of coded impulses passed through either the running rails or track-mounted cable loops and picked up by inductive coils on the train. On some high-speed passenger lines the ATP system obviates use of traditional trackside signals.

Among other automatic aids to railroad operation is the infrared "hotbox detector," which, located at trackside, detects the presence of an overheated wheel bearing and alerts the train crew. The modern hotbox detector identifies the location in the train of the overheating and, employing synthesized voice recording, radios the details to the train crew. Broken flange detectors are used in major terminals to indicate the presence of damaged wheels. Dragging equipment detectors warn crews if a car's brake rigging or other component is dragging on the track.

INTERLOCKING AND ROUTING

The first attempts at interlocking switches and signals were made in France in 1855 and in Britain in 1856. Interlocking at crossings and junctions prevents the displaying of a clear signal for one route when clearance has already been given to a train on a conflicting route. Route-setting or route-interlocking systems are modern extensions of this principle. With them the signaling operator or dispatcher can set up a complete route through a complicated track area by simply pushing buttons on a control panel. Most interlockings employ electrical relays, but adoption of computer-based solid-state interlocking began in Europe and Japan in the 1980s. Safeguard against malfunction is obtained by duplication or triplication; parallel computer systems are arranged to examine electronic route-setting commands in different ways, and only if automatic comparison shows no discrepancy in their proof that conflicting routes have been secured will the apparatus set the required route.

Electronics have greatly widened the scope for precise but at the same time labour-saving control of a busy railroad's traffic by making it possible to oversee extensive areas from one signaling or dispatching centre. This development is widely known as centralized traffic control (CTC). In Britain, for example, one signaling centre can cover more than 200 miles (320 km) of route with a principal city at the hub; the layout under control—used by intercity passenger, suburban passenger, and freight trains—may include 450 switch points and 1,200 possible route-settings. In the United States, the Union Pacific Railroad Company has consolidated dispatching control of its entire system in a single centre at its Omaha, Neb., headquarters. This concentration of signal and point control is possible because of the electronic ability to convey over a single communications channel a multitude of split-second, individually coded commands to ground apparatus and to return confirmations of compliance equally rapidly.

The functions of track circuits have been multiplied by electronics. The individual timetable number or alpha-numeric code of a train is entered into the signaling system at the track-circuited block where the train starts its journey. As the train moves from one block section to another, its occupation of successive track circuits automatically causes its number or code to move accordingly from one miniature illuminated window to another on the signaling centre's layout displays. When the train moves from one control area to another, its code will automatically move to the next centre's layout display. The real-time data on individual train progress generated by this system can be adapted for transmission to any interested railway office or, on a passenger railroad, to drive service information displays at stations. Particularly on rapid-transit systems, setting of junctions can be automated if train numbers or codes include an indication of routing, which is electronically detected when they occupy a track circuit at the approach to the divergence.

From the foregoing it is apparent that the means for complete automation of train operation exist. It has been applied to some private industrial rail systems since the early 1970s, and most of the capability has been built into some city metro systems. Extension of computer processing to the real-time data on train movement generated from track circuitry has further benefited control of major railroads' traffic. In Europe's latest centres controlling intensive passenger operations, operators can call up graphic video comparisons of actual train performance with schedule, projections of likely conflict at junctions where trains are not running on schedule, and recommendations for revision of train priorities to minimize disruption of scheduled operation. In North America, where many main lines are single-track, the Computer-Assisted Dispatching System (CADS) can relieve the operator of much routine work. At Union Pacific's Omaha centre, once the dispatcher has entered a train's identity and priority, the system automatically routes it accordingly, arranging its passing of other trains in loops as befits its priority. CADS automatically updates and modifies its determinations based on actual train movements and changing track conditions. The operator can intervene and override the system.

In early CTC installations the layout under a centre's control was shown only on one panoramic display, in which appropriately located lights indicated the setting of each switch point and signal, the track-circuited sections occupied by trains, and in windows at each occupied section the identifying code of the train in question. In some installations route-setting buttons were incorporated in this display. In the most recent CTC centres the overall panoramic display is generally retained, but operators have colour video screens portraying close-ups of the areas under their specific control. In many such cases, a light-pencil or tracker-ball movement of a cursor is used to identify on the screen the route to be changed. Alternatively, the operators may have alphanumeric keyboards on which reset route codes may be entered.

On the main lines of North America, precise control of train movement is more difficult than in Europe, because block sections are much longer. To overcome the problem, the principal railroads of the United States and Canada combined in the 1980s to develop an Advanced Train Control Systems (ATCS) project, which integrated

THE AUTOMATED HUMP YARD

A major area for automation techniques in railroading is the large classification, or marshaling, yard. In such yards, freight cars from many different origins are sorted out and placed in new trains going to the appropriate destinations. Marshaling yards are frequently called "hump yards" because the large installations have a hump over which cars are pushed. The cars then roll down from the hump by gravity, and each is routed into a classification or "bowl" track corresponding to its destination or where the train for the next stage of its transit is being formed.

Operations in classification yards has reached a high degree of automation. The heart of the yard is a central computer, into which is fed information concerning all cars in the yard or en route to it. As the cars are pushed up the hump (in some yards, by locomotives that are crewless and under remote radio control from the yard's operations centre), electronic scanners confirm their identity by means of a light-reflective label, place the data (car owner, number, and type) in a computer, and then set switches to direct each car into the proper bowl track. Electronic speed-control equipment measures such factors as the weight, speed, and rolling friction of each car and operates electric or electropneumatic "retarders" to control the speed of each car as it rolls down from the hump. Every phase of the yard's operations is monitored by a computerized management control and information system. With hand-held computers, ground staff can input data directly into the yard's central computer.

Because such electronically equipped yards can sort cars with great efficiency, they eliminate the need to do such work at other, smaller yards. Thus, one large electronic yard usually permits the closing or curtailing of a dozen or more other yards. Most modern electronic yards have quickly paid for themselves out of operating savings—and this takes no account of the benefits of improved service to shippers.

the potential of the latest microelectronics and communications technologies. In fully realized ATCS, trains continuously and automatically radio to the dispatching centre their exact location and speed; both would be determined by a locomotive-mounted scanner as well as signals received from global positioning system (GPS) satellites. In the dispatching centre, this input is processed to arrive at the optimal speed for each train in relation to its priority, the proximity of other trains it must pass, and route characteristics. From this analysis, continuously updated instructions can be radio-transmitted to train locomotives and processed by on-board computers for reproduction on cab displays so that trains can be driven with maximum regard for operating and fuel-consumption efficiency. ATCS can be developed in several stages, or levels, up to full implementation.

CHAPTER 6

THE ELEMENTS OF BRIDGE DESIGN

A bridge is a structure that spans horizontally between supports, whose function is to carry vertical loads. The prototypical bridge is quite simple—two supports holding up a beam—yet the engineering problems that must be overcome even in this simple form are inherent in every bridge: the supports must be strong enough to hold the structure up, and the span between supports must be strong enough to carry the loads. Spans are generally made as short as possible; long spans are justified where good foundations are limited—for example, over estuaries with deep water.

All major bridges are built with the public's money. Therefore, bridge design that best serves the public interest has a threefold goal: to be as efficient, as economical, and as elegant as is safely possible. Efficiency is a scientific principle that puts a value on reducing materials while increasing performance. Economy is a social principle that puts value on reducing the costs of construction and maintenance while retaining efficiency. Finally, elegance is a symbolic or visual principle that puts value on the personal expression of the designer without compromising performance or economy. There is little disagreement over what constitutes efficiency and economy, but the definition of elegance has always been controversial.

Modern designers have written about elegance or aesthetics since the early 19th century, beginning with the Scottish engineer Thomas Telford. Bridges ultimately belong to the general public, which is the final arbiter of

The multiple-span Seto Great Bridge over the Inland Sea, linking Kojima, Honshu, with Sakaide, Shikoku, Japan. Orion Press, Tokyo

this issue, but in general there are three positions taken by professionals. The first principle holds that the structure of a bridge is the province of the engineer and that beauty is fully achieved only by the addition of architecture. The second idea, arguing from the standpoint of pure engineering, insists that bridges making the most efficient possible use of materials are by definition beautiful. The third case holds that architecture is not needed but that engineers must think about how to make the structure beautiful. This last principle recognizes the fact that engineers have many possible choices of roughly equal efficiency and economy and can therefore express their own aesthetic ideas without adding significantly to materials or cost.

BASIC FORMS

There are six basic bridge forms: the beam, the truss, the arch, the suspension, the cantilever, and the cable-stay.

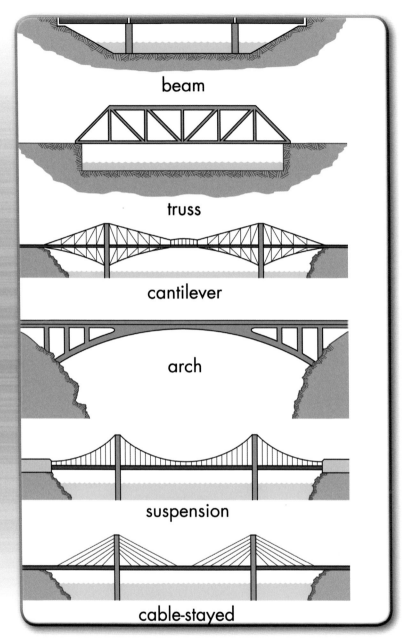

Six basic bridge forms. Encyclopædia Britannica, Inc.

BEAM

The beam bridge is the most common bridge form. A beam carries vertical loads by bending. As the beam bridge bends, it undergoes horizontal compression on the top. At the same time, the bottom of the beam is subjected to horizontal tension. The supports carry the loads from the beam by compression vertically to the foundations.

WORLD'S LONGEST-SPAN BEAM BRIDGES			MAIN SPAN		
BRIDGE	LOCATION	COMPLETED	METRES	FEET	NOTES
Steel truss					
Ikitsuki Ōhashi	Nagasaki prefecture, Japan	1991	400	1,312	Connects the islands of Iki and Hirado off northwestern Kyushu
Astoria	Astoria, Ore., U.S.	1966	375	1,232	Carries the Pacific Coast Highway across the Columbia River between Oregon and Washington
Francis Scott Key	Baltimore, Md., U.S.	1977	366	1,200	Spans the Patapsco River at Baltimore Harbor
Ōshima	Yamaguchi prefecture, Japan	1976	325	1,066	Links Yanai City and Ōshima Island

WORLD'S LONGEST-SPAN BEAM BRIDGES					
			MAIN SPAN		
BRIDGE	LOCATION	COMPLETED	METRES	FEET	NOTES
Tenmon	Kumamoto prefecture, Japan	1966	295	968	Part of Amakusa Gokyō (Five Bridges of Amakusa), linking islands in southwestern Kumamoto
Steel plate and box girder					
Presidente Costa e Silva	Rio de Janeiro state, Brazil	1974	300	984	Crosses Guanabara Bay between Rio de Janeiro and the suburb Niterói
Neckartalbrücke-1	Weitingen, Germany	1978	263	863	Carries a highway across the Neckar River valley
Brankova	Belgrade, Serbia, Serbia and Montenegro	1956	261	856	Provides a road crossing of the Sava River between Old and New Belgrade
Ponte de Vitória-3	Espírito Santo state, Brazil	1989	260	853	Provides a road link to the state capital on Vitória Island
Zoobrücke (Zoo Bridge)	Cologne, Germany	1966	259	850	Spans the Rhine River between the old city on the left bank and a convention centre on the right bank

When a bridge is made up of beams spanning between only two supports, it is called a simply supported beam bridge. If two or more beams are joined rigidly together over supports, the bridge becomes continuous.

TRUSS

A single-span truss bridge is like a simply supported beam because it carries vertical loads by bending. Bending leads to compression in the top chords (or horizontal members), tension in the bottom chords, and either tension or compression in the vertical and diagonal members, depending on their orientation. Trusses are popular because they use a relatively small amount of material to carry relatively large loads.

ARCH

WORLD'S LONGEST-SPAN ARCH BRIDGES					
			MAIN SPAN		
BRIDGE	**LOCATION**	**COMPLETED**	**METRES**	**FEET**	**NOTES**
Steel					
Lupu	Shanghai	2003	550	1,804	Crosses the Huangpu River between central Shanghai and Pudong New District
New River Gorge	Fayetteville, W.Va., U.S.	1977	518	1,700	Provides a road link through the scenic New River Gorge National River area

			MAIN SPAN		
BRIDGE	LOCATION	COMPLETED	METRES	FEET	NOTES
Bayonne	Bayonne, N.J., U.S.– New York City	1931	510	1,675	Spans the Kill Van Kull between New Jersey and Staten Island, New York
Sydney Harbour	Sydney, Australia	1932	503	1,650	Links the City of Sydney with North Sydney
Fremont	Portland, Ore., U.S.	1973	383	1,255	Links interstate highways over the Willamette River
Port Mann	Vancouver, B.C., Canada	1964	366	1,200	Carries the TransCanada Highway across the Fraser River
Concrete					
Wanxian	Sichuan province, China	1997	425	1,394	Crosses the Chang Jiang (Yangtze River) in the Three Gorges area
Krk I	Krk Island, Croatia	1980	390	1,279	Links scenic Krk Island with mainland Croatia
Jiangjiehe	Guizhou province, China	1995	330	1,082	Spans a gorge of the Wu River
Mike O'Callaghan– Pat Tillman Memorial Bridge	Boulder City, Nev., U.S.	2010	322	1,060	Spans the Colorado River at the Hoover Dam

Table title: WORLD'S LONGEST-SPAN ARCH BRIDGES

WORLD'S LONGEST-SPAN ARCH BRIDGES					
			MAIN SPAN		
BRIDGE	LOCATION	COMPLETED	METRES	FEET	NOTES
Yongning	Guangxi Autonomous Region, China	1996	312	1,023	Crosses the Yong River near Nanning
Gladesville	Sydney, Australia	1964	305	1,000	Spans the Parramatta River upstream from Sydney Harbour

The arch bridge carries loads primarily by compression, which exerts on the foundation both vertical and horizontal forces. Arch foundations must therefore prevent both vertical settling and horizontal sliding. In spite of the more complicated foundation design, the structure itself normally requires less material than a beam bridge of the same span.

SUSPENSION

WORLD'S LONGEST-SPAN SUSPENSION BRIDGES					
			MAIN SPAN		
BRIDGE	LOCATION	COMPLETED	METRES	FEET	NOTES
Akashi Strait	Kōbe–Awaji Island, Japan	1998	1,991	6,530	Part of the eastern link between the islands of Honshu and Shikoku

WORLD'S LONGEST-SPAN SUSPENSION BRIDGES

| | | | MAIN SPAN | | |
BRIDGE	LOCATION	COMPLETED	METRES	FEET	NOTES
Store Bælt (Great Belt)	Zealand-Funen, Denmark	1998	1,624	5,327	Part of the link between Copenhagen and mainland Europe
Humber	Near Hull, England	1981	1,410	4,625	Crosses the Humber estuary between Yorkshire and Lincolnshire, England
Jiangyin	Jiangsu province, China	1999	1,385	4,543	Crosses the Chang Jiang (Yangtze River) near Shanghai
Tsing Ma	Hong Kong	1997	1,377	4,517	Connects Hong Kong city with the airport on Landao Island
Verrazano-Narrows	New York City	1964	1,298	4,260	Spans New York Harbor between Brooklyn and Staten Island
Golden Gate	San Francisco	1937	1,280	4,200	Spans the entrance to San Francisco Bay

BRIDGE	LOCATION	COMPLETED	MAIN SPAN		NOTES
			METRES	**FEET**	
Höga Kusten (High Coast)	Kramfors, Sweden	1997	1,210	3,969	Crosses the Angerman River on a scenic coastal route in northern Sweden
Mackinac	Mackinaw City–St. Ignace, Mich., U.S.	1957	1,158	3,800	Spans the Straits of Mackinac between the Upper and Lower peninsulas of Michigan
Minami Bisan-Seto	Sakaide, Japan	1988	1,100	3,610	Part of the central link between the islands of Honshu and Shikoku
Bosporus II (Fatih Sultan Mehmed)	Istanbul	1988	1,090	3,576	Spans the strait from Rumeli Fortress on the European side to Anadolu Fortress on the Asian side

WORLD'S LONGEST-SPAN SUSPENSION BRIDGES

WORLD'S LONGEST-SPAN SUSPENSION BRIDGES					
			MAIN SPAN		
BRIDGE	LOCATION	COMPLETED	METRES	FEET	NOTES
9.844 pt	Istanbul	1973	1,074	3,523	Provides a highway link between European Turkey (Thrace) and Asian Turkey (Anatolia)
George Washington	New York City	1931	1,067	3,500	Crosses the Hudson River between New Jersey and Manhattan Island
Kurushima-3	Onomichi-Imabari, Japan	1999	1,030	3,378	Part of the western link between the islands of Honshu and Shikoku
Kurushima-2	Onomichi-Imabari, Japan	1999	1,020	3,346	Part of the western link between the islands of Honshu and Shikoku
Ponte 25 de Abril (Salazar)	Lisbon	1966	1,013	3,323	Provides the main cross-ing over the Tagus River into Lisbon

			MAIN SPAN		
BRIDGE	**LOCATION**	**COMPLETED**	**METRES**	**FEET**	**NOTES**
Forth Road	Queensferry, Scotland	1964	1,006	3,300	Carries automobile traffic over the Firth of Forth
Kita Bisan-Seto	Kojima-Sakaide, Japan	1988	990	3,248	Part of the central link between the islands of Honshu and Shikoku
Severn	Near Bristol, England	1966	988	3,240	Crosses the Severn estuary between England and Wales
Yichang	Hubei province, China	2001	960	3,149	Crosses the Chang Jiang (Yangtze River) downstream of Three Gorges Dam

WORLD'S LONGEST-SPAN SUSPENSION BRIDGES

A suspension bridge carries vertical loads through curved cables in tension. These loads are transferred both to the towers, which carry them by vertical compression to the ground, and to the anchorages, which must resist the inward and sometimes vertical pull of the cables. The suspension bridge can be viewed as an upside-down arch in tension with only the towers in compression. Because the deck is hung in the air, care must be taken to ensure that it does not move excessively under loading. The deck therefore must be either heavy or stiff or both.

CANTILEVER

			MAIN SPAN		
BRIDGE	LOCATION	COMPLETED	METRES	FEET	NOTES
Steel truss					
Pont de Québec	Quebec City, Que., Canada	1917	549	1,801	Provides a rail crossing over the St. Lawrence River
Forth	Queensferry, Scotland	1890	2 spans, each 521	2 spans, each 1,709	Provides a rail crossing over the Firth of Forth
Minato	Ōsaka-Amagasaki, Japan	1974	510	1,675	Carries road traffic across Ōsaka's harbour
Commodore John J. Barry	Bridgeport, N.J., U.S.–Chester, Pa., U.S.	1974	501	1,644	Provides a road crossing over the Delaware River

WORLD'S LONGEST-SPAN CANTILEVER BRIDGES

			MAIN SPAN		
BRIDGE	LOCATION	COMPLETED	METRES	FEET	NOTES

WORLD'S LONGEST-SPAN CANTILEVER BRIDGES

BRIDGE	LOCATION	COMPLETED	METRES	FEET	NOTES
Greater New Orleans-2	New Orleans, La., U.S.	1988	486	1,595	Provides parallel service to the Greater New Orleans-1 Bridge
Greater New Orleans-1	New Orleans, La., U.S.	1958	480	1,575	Connects highway traffic across the Mississippi River
Howrah	Kolkata, India	1943	457	1,500	Provides automobile and pedestrian crossings of the Hooghly River
Prestressed concrete					
Stolmasundet	Austevoll, Norway	1998	301	987	Links the islands of Stolmen and Sjelbörn south of Bergen
Raftsundet	Lofoten, Norway	1998	298	977	Crosses Raft Sound in the Lofoten islands

WORLD'S LONGEST-SPAN CANTILEVER BRIDGES			MAIN SPAN		
BRIDGE	LOCATION	COMPLETED	METRES	FEET	NOTES
Sundøy	Leirfjord, Norway	2003	298	977	Links Alsten Island to the mainland
Boca Tigris-2	Humen, China	1997	270	886	Part of a multispan link across Tiger's Mouth (Boca Tigris) of the Pearl River Delta
Gateway	Brisbane, Australia	1986	260	853	Provides a highway link between Queensland's Sunshine Coast and Gold Coast

A beam is said to be cantilevered when it projects outward, supported only at one end. A cantilever bridge is generally made with three spans, of which the outer spans are both anchored down at the shore and cantilever out over the channel to be crossed. The central span rests on the cantilevered arms extending from the outer spans; it carries vertical loads like a simply supported beam or a truss—that is, by tension forces in the lower chords and compression in the upper chords. The cantilevers carry their loads by tension in the upper chords and compression in the lower ones. Inner towers carry those forces by compression to the foundation, and outer towers carry the forces by tension to the far foundations.

CABLE-STAY

			MAIN SPAN		
BRIDGE	LOCATION	COMPLETED	METRES	FEET	NOTES
Sutong	Jiangsu province, China	2008	1,088	3,570	Crosses Chang Jiang (Yangtze River) between Suzhou and Nantong
Tatara	Onomichi-Imabari, Japan	1999	890	2,919	Part of the western link between the islands of Honshu and Shikoku
Normandie	near Le Havre, France	1995	856	2,808	Crosses the Seine estuary between Haute- and Basse-Normandie
Nancha	Nanjing, China	2001	628	2,060	Southern span of the Second Nanjing Yangtze Bridge
Wuhan Baishazhou	Hubei province, China	2000	618	2,027	Provides the third crossing of the Chang Jiang (Yangtze River) in the city of Wuhan
Qingzhou Minjiang	Fuzhou, China	2001	605	1,984	Connects Fuzhou with the airport across the Min River

Table title: **WORLD'S LONGEST-SPAN CABLE-STAYED BRIDGES**

			MAIN SPAN		
BRIDGE	LOCATION	COMPLETED	METRES	FEET	NOTES
Xupu	Shanghai	1997	590	1,935	Crosses the Huangpu River between southwestern Shanghai and Pudong New District
Meiko Chuo (Meiko Central)	Nagoya, Japan	1998	590	1,935	Middle of three spans crossing Nagoya's port
Skarnsundet	Near Trondheim, Norway	1991	530	1,738	Crosses scenic Trondheimsfjorden between northern and southern Norway
Queshi	Shantou, China	1998	518	1,699	Carries highway traffic across Shantou's harbour
Tsurumi Tsubasa	Yokohama, Japan	1994	510	1,673	One of two spans crossing Yokohama's harbour
Jingsha	Hubei province, China	2002	500	1,640	Part of a multi-span crossing of the Jingsha River (upper Chang Jiang [upper Yangtze River]) on a north-south national highway
Ikuchi	Onomichi-Imabari, Japan	1991	490	1,607	Part of the western link between the islands of Honshu and Shikoku

The title of the table is: **WORLD'S LONGEST-SPAN CABLE-STAYED BRIDGES**

| | | | MAIN SPAN | | |
BRIDGE	LOCATION	COMPLETED	METRES	FEET	NOTES
Øresund (Öresund)	Copenhagen–Malmö, Sweden	2000	490	1,607	Part of the link across The Sound between Denmark and Sweden

WORLD'S LONGEST-SPAN CABLE-STAYED BRIDGES

Cable-stayed bridges carry the vertical main-span loads by nearly straight diagonal cables in tension. The towers transfer the cable forces to the foundations through vertical compression. The tensile forces in the cables also put the deck into horizontal compression.

MATERIALS

The four primary materials used for bridges have been wood, stone, iron, and concrete. Of these, iron has had the greatest effect on modern bridges. From iron, steel is made, and steel is used to make reinforced and prestressed concrete. Modern bridges are almost exclusively built with steel, reinforced concrete, and prestressed concrete.

WOOD AND STONE

Wood is relatively weak in both compression and tension, but it has almost always been widely available and inexpensive. Wood has been used effectively for small bridges that carry light loads, such as footbridges. Engineers now incorporate laminated wooden beams and arches into some modern bridges.

Stone is strong in compression but weak in tension. Its primary application has been in arches, piers, and abutments.

IRON AND STEEL

The first iron used during the Industrial Revolution was cast iron, which is strong in compression but weak in tension. Wrought iron, on the other hand, is as strong in compression as cast iron, but it also has much greater tensile strength. Steel is an even further refinement of iron and is yet stronger, superior to any iron in both tension and compression. Steel can be made to varying strengths, some alloys being five times stronger than others. The engineer refers to these as high-strength steels.

CONCRETE

Concrete is an artificial stone made from a mixture of water, sand, gravel, and a binder such as cement. Like stone, it is strong in compression and weak in tension. Concrete with steel bars embedded in it is called reinforced concrete. Reinforcement allows for less concrete to be used because the steel carries all the tension; also, the concrete protects the steel from corrosion and fire.

Prestressed concrete is an important variation of reinforced concrete. A typical process, called post-tensioned prestressing, involves casting concrete beams with longitudinal holes for steel tendons—cables or bars—like reinforced concrete, but the holes for the tendons are curved upward from end to end, and the tendons, once fitted inside, are stretched and then anchored at the ends. The tendons, now under high tension, pull the two anchored ends together, putting the beam into compression. In addition, the curved tendons exert an upward force, and the designer can make this upward force counteract much of the downward load expected to be carried by the beam. Prestressed concrete reduces the amount of steel and concrete needed in a structure, leading to lighter designs that are often less expensive than designs of reinforced concrete.

CONSTRUCTION

The methods employed to construct a bridge depend on the bridge's form—that is, on whether it is a beam, truss, arch, suspension, cantilever, or cable-stay bridge.

BEAM BRIDGES

All bridges need to be secure at the foundations and abutments. In the case of a typical overpass beam bridge with one support in the middle, construction begins with the casting of concrete footings for the pier and abutments. Where the soil is especially weak, wooden or steel piles are driven to support the footings. After the concrete piers and abutments have hardened sufficiently, the erection of a concrete or steel superstructure begins. Steel beams are generally made in a factory, shipped to the site, and set in place by cranes. For short spans, steel beams are usually formed as a single unit. At the site, they are placed parallel to each other, with temporary forms between them so that a concrete deck can be cast on top. The beams usually have metal pieces welded on their top flanges, around which the concrete is poured. These pieces provide a connection between beam and slab, thus producing a composite structure.

For longer spans, steel beams are made in the form of plate girders. A plate girder is an I beam consisting of separate top and bottom flanges welded or bolted to a vertical web. While beams for short spans are usually of a constant depth, beams for longer spans are often haunched—that is, deeper at the supports and shallower at mid-span. Haunching stiffens the beam at the supports, thereby reducing bending at mid-span.

ARCH BRIDGES

Arches are normally fabricated on-site. After the building of abutments (and piers, if the bridge is multiarch), a falsework is constructed. For a concrete arch, metal or wooden falsework and forms hold the cast concrete and are later removed. For steel arches, a cantilevering method is standard. Each side of an arch is built out toward the other, supported by temporary cables above or by falsework below until the ends meet. At this point the arch becomes self-supporting, and the cables or falsework are removed.

SUSPENSION BRIDGES

When bridges requiring piers are built over a body of water, foundations are made by sinking caissons into the riverbed and filling them with concrete. Caissons are large boxes or cylinders that have been made from wood, metal, or concrete. In the case of suspension bridges, towers are built atop the caissons. The first suspension-bridge towers were stone, but now they are either steel or concrete. Next, the anchorages are built on both ends, usually of reinforced concrete with embedded steel eyebars to which the cables will be fastened. An eyebar is a length of metal with a hole (or "eye") at the ends. Cables for the first suspension bridges were made of linked wrought-iron eyebars; now, however, cables are generally made of thousands of steel wires spun together at the construction site. Spinning is done by rope pulleys that carry each wire across the top of the towers to the opposite anchorage and back. The wires are then bundled and covered to prevent corrosion. When the cables are complete, suspenders are hung, and finally the deck is erected—usually by floating deck sections out on ships, hoisting them with cranes, and securing them to the suspenders.

CANTILEVER BRIDGES

Like suspension bridges, steel cantilever bridges generally carry heavy loads over water, so their construction begins with the sinking of caissons and the erection of towers and anchorages. For steel cantilever bridges, the steel frame is built out from the towers toward the centre and the abutments. When a shorter central span is required, it is usually floated out and raised into place. The deck is added last.

Construction of the Forth Railway Bridge, designed by Sir John Fowler and Sir Benjamin Baker on the cantilever principle, crossing the Firth of Forth in Scotland, c. 1860s. © Photos.com/Thinkstock

The cantilever method for erecting prestressed concrete bridges consists of building a concrete cantilever in short segments, prestressing each succeeding segment onto the earlier ones. Each new segment is supported by the previous segment while it is being cast, thus avoiding the need for falsework.

THE FORTH BRIDGE

One of the first cantilever bridges (and for several years the world's longest span) was a railway bridge over the Firth of Forth, the estuary of the Forth River in Scotland. It was designed and built in the late 1880s by Benjamin Baker, an English civil engineer who had bored tunnels for the London Underground lines and built docks at Avonmouth and Hull. Making use of the rocky isle of Inchgarvie in the middle of the deep firth as a foundation for one of three giant (1,350-foot [411-metre]) cantilevers (projecting members supported at only one end), Baker joined the cantilevers together with two suspended spans of 350 feet (107 metres) each, making a total of 1,700 feet (518 metres) of clear span over either arm of the firth. The 12-foot- (4-metre-) diameter tubes forming the cantilevers, the roadway, and approach spans consumed the hitherto unheard-of quantity of 58,000 tons of steel. The cost of the bridge, extraordinary for its day, was £3 million (about $15 million).

At its opening in 1890, the bridge stirred great controversy on aesthetic grounds. The poet and artist William Morris declared it "the supremest specimen of all ugliness"—a judgment greatly softened by the passage of time, for the bridge, although appearing dense and massive from an approaching point of view, exhibits a surprising lightness in profile. Today it is considered to be one of the greatest engineering feats of all time.

CABLE-STAYED BRIDGES

Construction of cable-stayed bridges usually follows the cantilever method. After the tower is built, one cable and a section of the deck are constructed in each direction.

Each section of the deck is prestressed before continuing. The process is repeated until the deck sections meet in the middle, where they are connected. The ends are anchored at the abutments.

PERFORMANCE IN SERVICE

Bridges are designed, first, to carry their own permanent weight, or dead load; second, to carry traffic, or live

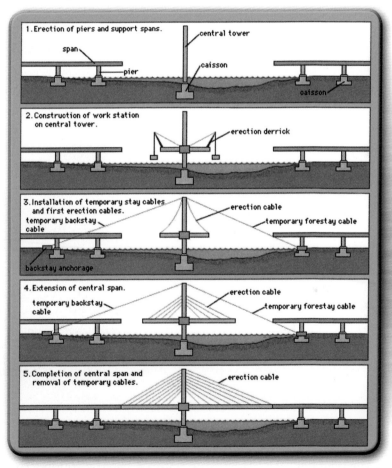

1. Erection of piers and support spans.
central tower
span
pier
caisson
caisson

2. Construction of work station on central tower.
erection derrick

3. Installation of temporary stay cables and first erection cables.
temporary backstay cable
erection cable
temporary forestay cable
backstay anchorage

4. Extension of central span.
temporary backstay cable
erection cable
temporary forestay cable

5. Completion of central span and removal of temporary cables.
erection cable

Five steps in the cantilever-method construction of a cable-stayed bridge. © Encyclopædia Britannica; rendering for this edition by Rosen Educational Services

loads; and, finally, to resist natural forces such as winds or earthquakes.

LIVE LOAD AND DEAD LOAD

The primary function of a bridge is to carry traffic loads: heavy trucks, cars, and trains. Engineers must estimate the traffic loading. On short spans, it is possible that the maximum conceivable load will be achieved—that is to say, on spans of less than 100 feet (30 metres), four heavy trucks may cross at the same time, two in each direction. On longer spans of a thousand metres or more, the maximum conceivable load is such a remote possibility (imagine the Golden Gate Bridge with only heavy trucks crossing bumper-to-bumper in each direction at the same time) that the cost of designing for it is unreasonable. Therefore, engineers use probable loads as a basis for design.

In order to carry traffic, the structure must have some weight, and on short spans this dead load weight is usually less than the live loads. On longer spans, however, the dead load is greater than live loads, and, as spans get longer, it becomes more important to design forms that minimize dead load. In general, shorter spans are built with beams, hollow boxes, trusses, arches, and continuous versions of the same, while longer spans use cantilever, cable-stay, and suspension forms. As spans get longer, questions of shape, materials, and form become increasingly important. New forms have evolved to provide longer spans with more strength from less material.

FORCES OF NATURE

Dead and live weight are essentially vertical loads, whereas forces from nature may be either vertical or horizontal.

Wind causes two important loads, one called static and the other dynamic. Static wind load is the horizontal pressure that tries to push a bridge sideways. Dynamic wind load gives rise to vertical motion, creating oscillations in any direction. Like the breaking of an overused violin string, oscillations are vibrations that can cause a bridge to fail. If a deck is thin and not properly shaped and supported, it may experience dangerous vertical or torsional (twisting) movements.

The expansion and contraction of bridge materials by heat and cold have been minimized by the use of expansion joints in the deck along with bearings at the abutments and at the tops of piers. Bearings allow the bridge to react to varying temperatures without causing detrimental stress to the material. In arches, engineers sometimes design hinges to reduce stresses caused by temperature movement.

Modern bridges must also withstand natural disasters such as tropical cyclones and earthquakes. In general, earthquakes are best withstood by structures that carry as light a dead weight as possible, because the horizontal forces that arise from ground accelerations are proportional to the weight of the structure. (This phenomenon is explained by the fundamental Newtonian law of force equals mass times acceleration.) For cyclones, it is generally best that the bridge be aerodynamically designed to have little solid material facing the winds so that they may pass through or around the bridge without setting up dangerous oscillations.

I ndustrial strength has been an important factor in the evolution of bridges. Great Britain, the leading industrialized country of the early 19th century, built the most significant bridges of that time. Likewise, innovations arose in the United States from the late 19th century through the mid-20th century and in Japan and Germany in subsequent decades. Switzerland, with its highly industrialized society, has also been a fertile ground for advances in bridge building.

IRON AND STEEL, 1779–1929

Truly modern bridges began with the introduction of industrially produced iron, which can be dated for convenience to the Ironbridge of Coalbrookdale, Eng., built in 1779. They evolved over the following 150 years as engineers came to understand better the new possibilities inherent first in cast iron, then in wrought iron and structural steel. This evolution can be seen as reaching its greatest expression in the steel suspension bridges of the early 20th century.

IRON

During the Industrial Revolution the timber and masonry tradition was eclipsed by the use of iron, which was stronger than stone and usually less costly.

EARLY DESIGNS

The first bridge built solely of iron spanned the Severn River near Coalbrookdale, Eng. Designed by Thomas Pritchard and built in 1779 by Abraham Darby, the Ironbridge, constructed of cast-iron pieces, is a ribbed arch whose nearly semicircular 100-foot (30-metre) span imitates stone construction by exploiting the strength of cast iron in compression. In 1795 the Severn region was wracked by disastrous floods, and the Ironbridge, lacking the wide flat surfaces of stone structures, allowed the floodwaters to pass through it. It was the only bridge in the region to survive—a fact noted by the Scottish engineer Thomas Telford, who then began to create a series of iron bridges that were judged to be technically the best of their time. The 1814 Craigellachie Bridge, over the Spey River in Scotland, is the oldest surviving metal bridge of Telford's. Its 150-foot (45-metre) arch has a flat, nearly parabolic profile made up of two curved arches connected by X-bracing. The roadway has a slight vertical curve and is supported by thin diagonal members that carry loads to the arch.

The use of relatively economical wrought iron freed up the imaginations of designers, and one of the first results was Telford's use of chain suspension cables to carry loads by tension. His eyebar cables consisted of wrought-iron bars of 20 to 30 feet (6 to 9 metres) with holes at each end. Each eye matched the eye on another bar, and the two were linked by iron pins. The first of these major chain-suspension bridges and the finest of its day was Telford's Menai Bridge, over the Menai Strait in northwestern Wales. At the time of its completion in 1826, its 580-foot (174-metre) span was the world's longest. In 1893 its timber deck was replaced with a steel deck, and in 1940 steel

The Royal Albert Bridge (1859) over the Tamar River at Saltash, Eng., designed by Isambard Kingdom Brunel. © Photos.com/Jupiterimages

chains replaced the corroded wrought-iron ones. The bridge is still in service today.

RAILWAY BRIDGES

The rise of the locomotive as a mode of transportation during the 19th century spurred the design of new bridges and bridge forms strong enough to handle both the increased weight and the dynamic loads of trains. The most significant of these early railway bridges was Robert Stephenson's Britannia Bridge, also over the Menai Straits. Completed in 1850, Stephenson's design was the first to employ the hollow box girder. The hollow box gave the deck the extra stiffness of a truss, but it was easier to build and required less engineering precision—at the cost, however, of extra material. The wrought-iron boxes through which the trains ran were originally to be carried by chain suspension cables, but, during the building, extensive theoretical work and testing indicated that the cables were not needed; thus the towers stand strangely useless.

For the Royal Albert Bridge (1859) over the Tamar River at Saltash, Eng., designer Isambard Kingdom Brunel used a combination of tubular arch and chain cable. The arches rise above the deck and, in conjunction with the chain suspenders, gives the bridge in profile what appear to be a set of eyes. The bridge at Saltash also carries trains, and its two main spans of 455 feet (136.5 metres) are comparable in length to the Britannia's 460-foot (138-metre) spans.

Among the most important railway bridges of the latter 19th century were those of Gustave Eiffel. Between 1867 and 1869 Eiffel constructed four viaducts of trussed-girder design along the rail line between Gannat and Commentry, west of Vichy in France. The most striking of these, at Rouzat, features wrought-iron towers that for the first time visibly reflect the need for lateral stiffness to counter the influence of horizontal wind loads. Lateral stiffness is achieved by curving the towers out at the base where they meet the masonry foundations, a design style that culminated in Eiffel's famous Parisian tower of 1889.

Eiffel also designed two major arch bridges that were the longest-spanning structures of their type at the time. The first, the 1877 Pia Maria Bridge over the Duoro River near Oporto, Portugal, is a 522-foot (157-metre), crescent-shaped span that rises 140 feet (42 metres) at its crown. Again, a wide spreading of the arches at their base gives this structure greater lateral stiffness.

The crowning achievement of the crescent-arch form in the 19th century was represented by the completion in 1884 of Eiffel's 541-foot (162-metre) Garabit Viaduct over the Truyère River near Saint-Flour, France. Unlike the bridge at Duoro, the Garabit arch is separated visually from the thin horizontal girder. Both arches were

THE BRITANNIA BRIDGE

The Britannia Bridge is a railroad bridge in northern Wales spanning Menai Strait, between Bangor and the Isle of Anglesey. It was designed and built by Robert Stephenson, who, with his father, George Stephenson, built the first successful locomotive. Unable to use an arch design because the Admiralty would not allow the strait to be closed to the passage of sailing ships, Stephenson conceived the idea of using a pair of completely enclosed iron tubes, rectangular in section, supported in the centre by a pier built on Britannia Rock. William Fairbairn carried out a series of metallurgical tests, and from 1846 to 1849 the work was executed, the iron tubes being floated into position and lifted by capstan and hydraulic power. The bridge, which carried the London–Holyhead railway across the strait, was severely damaged by fire in 1970. During the repairs, the tubes were replaced by concrete decks—one for the railway, a second for motor traffic—supported by steel arches.

designed with hinges at their supports so that the crescent shape widens from points at the supports to a deep but light truss at the crown. The hinged design served to facilitate construction and also to produce the powerful visual image intended by Eiffel.

SUSPENSION BRIDGES

In the United States, engineer John Roebling established a factory in 1841 for making rope out of iron wire, which he initially sold to replace the hempen rope used for hoisting cars over the portage railway in central Pennsylvania. Later Roebling used wire ropes as suspension cables for bridges, and he developed the technique for spinning the cables in place rather than making a prefabricated cable that needed to be lifted into place. In 1855 Roebling completed an 821-foot- (246-metre-) span railway bridge over the Niagara River in western New

York state. Wind loads were not yet understood in any theoretical sense, but Roebling recognized the practical need to prevent vertical oscillations. He therefore added numerous wire stays, which extended like a giant spiderweb in various directions from the deck to the valley below and to the towers above. The Niagara Bridge confounded nearly all the engineering judgment of the day, which held that suspension bridges could not sustain railway traffic. Although the trains were required to slow down to a speed of only 3 miles (5 km) per hour and repairs were frequent, the bridge was in service for 42 years, and it was replaced only because newer trains had become too heavy for it.

Roebling's Cincinnati Bridge (now called the John A. Roebling Bridge) over the Ohio River was a prototype for his masterful Brooklyn Bridge. When this 1,057-foot- (317-metre-) span, iron-wire cable suspension bridge was completed in 1866, it was the longest spanning bridge in the world. Roebling's mature style showed itself in the structure's impressive stone towers and its thin suspended span, with stays radiating from the tower tops to control deck oscillations from wind loads.

STEEL

Steel, an alloy of iron and carbon, is a material ideally suited for building the world's infrastructure and industries. Possessing an unparalleled range of mechanical properties, it is made of two relatively cheap raw materials (iron ore and scrap), and it is relatively easy to make, form, and process. Bulk steel production was made possible by the English engineer Henry Bessemer in 1855, when he obtained British patents for a pneumatic steelmaking process. The effects on construction, including bridge construction, were seen almost immediately.

RAILWAY BRIDGES

Between the American Civil War and World War I, railroads reached their peak in the United States and elsewhere, increasing the need for bridges that could withstand these heavier loads. New processes for making steel gave rise to many important bridges, such as the Eads Bridge over the Mississippi River at St. Louis, the Forth Bridge over the Firth of Forth in Scotland, the Hell Gate Bridge and Bayonne Bridge in New York City, and the Sydney Harbour Bridge in Australia.

The 1874 Eads Bridge was the first major bridge built entirely of steel, excluding the pier foundations. Designed by James Buchanan Eads, it has three arch spans, of which the two sides are each 502 feet (151 metres) and the middle is 520 feet (156 metres). The Eads Bridge was given added strength by its firm foundations, for which pneumatic caissons, instead of cofferdams, were used for the first time in the United States. Another innovation carried out by Eads, based on a proposal by Telford, was the construction of arches by the cantilevering method. The arches were held up by cables supported by temporary towers above the piers, all of which were removed when the arches became self-supporting.

The Forth Bridge over the Firth of Forth in Scotland, designed by Benjamin Baker, has two cantilevered spans of 1,710 feet (513 metres), which made it the world's longest bridge upon its completion in 1890. The steel structure rises 342 feet (103 metres) above the masonry piers. Baker designed the bridge with an artist's temperament. In his writings he criticized the Britannia Bridge for its towers, which Stephenson admitted had been left in place only in case the bridge needed suspension chains and not out of structural necessity. The Forth Bridge, on the other hand, is pure structure; nothing has been added for aesthetic appearance that does not have a structural function. For more than a century the bridge has carried a railway, and indeed it was one of the last great bridges built for that purpose in the 19th century.

The Hell Gate Bridge, completed by Gustav Lindenthal in 1916, also had an aesthetic intention. It was made to look massive by its stone towers and by the increased spacing of the two chords at the support, yet structurally the towers serve no purpose; the lower chord of the arch is actually hinged at the abutments, and all of the load is carried to the foundations by that lower chord. Nevertheless, the bridge has an imposing presence, and its arch of 978 feet (293 metres) was the world's longest at the time.

Similar in arch form to Hell Gate is the 1931 Bayonne Bridge, designed by Lindenthal's former associate, Othmar Ammann. Spanning the Kill van Kull between Staten Island, New York, and Bayonne, New Jersey, the Bayonne Bridge, though longer than the Hell Gate Bridge at 1,652 feet (496 metres), is significantly lighter. The main span for the Hell Gate required 87 million pounds (39 million kg) of steel, compared with 37 million pounds (17 million kg) for the Bayonne. Part of the reason is the lower live loads; for the Hell Gate, train loading was taken at 24,000 pounds per foot (36,000 kg per metre) of bridge length, whereas for the Bayonne the car loading was 7,000 pounds per foot (10,000 kg per metre). But the decrease is also due to an effort to make the arch more graceful as well as more economical. Massive-looking stone-faced abutments were designed for the sake of appearance but then were never built, leaving a rather useless tangle of light steel latticework at the abutments. Nevertheless, from a distance the Bayonne Bridge shows a lightness and delicacy that bespeaks structural integrity.

Across the world in Sydney Harbour, New South Wales, Australia, Sir Ralph Freeman designed a steel arch bridge

Workmen wrapping wire around a suspension cable of the Brooklyn Bridge, New York; wood engraving published 1883. © Photos.com/Thinkstock

with a span of 1,650 feet (495 metres) that was begun in 1924 and completed in 1932. Because of the deep waters in the harbour, temporary supports were impractical, so the steel arch was assembled by cantilevering out from each bank and meeting in the middle. A high-strength silicon steel was used, making it the heaviest steelwork of its kind. The Sydney Harbour Bridge is a two-hinged arch, with its deck 172 feet (52 metres) above the water. It carries railroad tracks, a roadway 57 feet (17 metres) wide, and two walkways. On each bank it is supported by a pair of large stone towers that, like those of the Hell Gate, disguise the fact that almost the entire load is carried by the lower arch chord.

SUSPENSION BRIDGES

John Roebling died in 1869, shortly after work began on the Brooklyn Bridge, but the project was taken over and seen to completion by his son, Washington Roebling, and Washington's wife, Emily Warren Roebling. Technically, the bridge overcame many obstacles through the use of huge pneumatic caissons, into which compressed air was pumped so that men could work in the dry; but, more important, it was the first suspension bridge on which steel wire was used for the cables. Every wire was galvanized to safeguard against rust, and the four cables, each nearly 16 inches (40 cm) in diameter, took 26 months to spin back and forth over the East River. After many political and technical difficulties and at least 27 fatal accidents, the 1,595-foot- (479-metre-) span bridge was completed in 1883 to such fanfare that within 24 hours an estimated quarter-million people crossed over it, using a central elevated walkway that John Roebling had designed for the purpose of giving pedestrians a dramatic view of the city.

By the turn of the 20th century, the increased need for passage from Manhattan to Brooklyn over the East River resulted in plans for two more long-span, wire-cable, steel suspension bridges, the Williamsburg and Manhattan bridges. The Williamsburg Bridge, designed by L.L. Buck with a span of just over 1,600 feet (480 metres), became the longest cable-suspension span in the world upon completion in 1903. Its deck truss is a bulky lattice structure with a depth of 40 feet (12 metres), and the towers are of steel rather than masonry. The truss in effect replaced Roebling's stays as stiffeners for the deck.

The 1909 Manhattan Bridge has a span of 1,470 feet (441 metres). Its fixed steel towers spread laterally at the base, and a 24.5-foot- (7.4-metre-) deep truss is used for the deck. Of greater significance than the deck construction, however, was the first application of deflection theory, during the design of these two bridges, in calculating how the horizontal deck and curved cables worked together to carry loads. First published in 1888 by the Austrian academic Josef Melan, deflection theory explains how deck and cables deflect together under gravity loads so that, as spans become longer and the suspended structure heavier, the required stiffness of the deck actually decreases. Deflection theory especially influenced design in the 1930s, as engineers attempted to reduce the ratio of girder depth to span length in order to achieve a lighter, more graceful, appearance without compromising safety. Up to 1930, no long-span suspension bridge had a ratio of girder depth to span length that was higher than 1:84.

Ralph Modjeski's Philadelphia-Camden Bridge (now called the Benjamin Franklin Bridge), over the Delaware River, is another wire-cable steel suspension bridge; when completed in 1926, it was the world's longest span at 1,750 feet (525 metres). However, it was soon exceeded by the Ambassador Bridge (1929) in Detroit and the George Washington Bridge (1931) in New York. The Ambassador links the United States and Canada over the Detroit River. Because of heavy traffic on the river, a wide clearance was necessary. The steel suspension bridge designed by Jonathan Jones has a span of 1,850 feet (555 metres) and a total length, including approach spans, of more than 9,000 feet (2,700 metres). The design of the Ambassador Bridge originally called for using heat-treated steel wires for the cables. Normally wires were cold-drawn, a method in which steel is drawn through successively smaller holes in dies, reducing its diameter yet raising its ultimate tensile strength. Extensive laboratory tests showed that heat-treated wires had a slightly higher ultimate strength, but during the construction of the Ambassador Bridge several of them broke, and, to the contractors' credit, all the cables spun thus far were immediately replaced with cold-drawn wire. The example illustrates the limitations of laboratory testing as opposed to studies of actual working conditions.

The George Washington Bridge, a steel suspension bridge designed by Ammann, was significant first for its span length of 3,500 feet (1,050 metres) and second for its theoretical innovations. After studying deflection theory, Ammann concluded that no stiffness was needed in the deck at all, as it would be stabilized by the great weight of the bridge itself. Indeed, the George Washington Bridge became the heaviest single-span suspension bridge in the world at the time of its completion, and its original ratio of girder depth to span was an astonishing 1:350. Originally the 635-foot- (191-metre-) high towers were to have a masonry facade, but a shortage of money during the Great Depression precluded this, and the steel framework stands alone. Ammann designed the bridge to carry a maximum of 8,000 pounds per foot (12,000 kg per metre), even though the maximum conceivable load on the bridge was estimated at 46,000 pounds per foot (69,000 kg per metre), thus illustrating the principle that longer bridges need not be designed for maximum load. In 1962 the addition of a second deck for traffic resulted in the construction of a deck truss, giving the bridge its current ratio of girder depth to span of 1:120.

THE FIRST CONCRETE BRIDGES

Concrete is an aggregate of sand and gravel that is bonded together by cement and water. Because of its potential for immense strength and its initial ability to adapt to virtually

THE BROOKLYN BRIDGE

A brilliant feat of 19th-century engineering, the Brooklyn Bridge was the first bridge to use steel for cable wire, and during its construction explosives were used inside a pneumatic caisson for the first time.

Brooklyn Bridge, with a view of New York City, 1898. Library of Congress, Washington, D.C.

The masterwork of John Augustus Roebling, the bridge was built (1869–83) in the face of immense difficulties. Roebling died as a result of an accident at the outset, and his son, Washington Roebling, after taking over as chief engineer, suffered a crippling attack of decompression sickness (caisson disease) during the founding of the New York pier (1872). Confined to his apartment in Columbia Heights (Brooklyn), he continued to direct operations, observing with field glasses and sending messages to the site by his wife, Emily Warren Roebling. A compressed-air blast that wrecked a pneumatic caisson slowed the work, as did a severe fire that smoldered for weeks in another caisson, a cable that parted from its anchorage on the Manhattan side and crashed into the river, and the fraud perpetrated by a steel-wire contractor that necessitated the replacement of tons of cable. At least 20 workers were killed during construction, and many more suffered decompression sickness.

The Brooklyn Bridge's 1,595-foot (486-metre) main span was the longest in the world until the completion of the Firth of Forth cantilever bridge in Scotland in 1890. Its deck, supported by four cables, carries both automobile and pedestrian traffic. A distinctive feature is the broad promenade above the roadway, which John Roebling accurately predicted "in a crowded commercial city will be of incalculable value."

The bridge's opening day (May 24, 1883) was marked by much celebration, and the building of it came to represent a landmark in technological achievement for a generation. Its strength and grace inspired poets, notably Walt Whitman, Hart Crane, and Marianne Moore, and a legion of photographers and painters, including Joseph Stella, John Marin, Berenice Abbott, and Alfred Eisenstaedt.

any form, it has become one of the most common building materials in the world. With the arrival of steel-reinforced and prestressed concrete in the late 19th and early 20th centuries, bridge designs finally broke completely with the designs in wood or stone that characterized bridges before the Industrial Revolution.

REINFORCED CONCRETE

During the 19th century, low-cost production of iron and steel, when added to the invention of portland cement in 1824, led to the development of reinforced concrete. In 1867 a French gardener, Joseph Monier, patented a method of strengthening thin concrete flowerpots by embedding iron wire mesh into the concrete. Monier later applied his ideas to patents for buildings and bridges. In 1879 another Frenchman, François Hennebique, set out to fire-proof a metal-frame house in Belgium, and his decision to cover the iron beams with concrete led him to develop a structural system wherein the metal bars (replacing iron beams) carried tension and the concrete carried compression. By the end of the century reinforced concrete had become an economical substitute for stone, since it was generally cheaper to produce concrete than to quarry stones. In addition to its price and load-carrying advantages, reinforced concrete could be molded into a variety of shapes, allowing for much aesthetic expression on the part of the engineer without significantly increasing materials or cost.

EARLY BRIDGES

The most prolific designers first using reinforced concrete were Hennebique and the German engineer G.A. Wayss, who bought the Monier patents. Hennebique's Vienne River Bridge at Châtellerault, France, built in 1899, was the longest-spanning reinforced arch bridge of the 19th century. Built low to the river—typical of many reinforced-concrete bridges whose goal of safe passage across a small river is not affected by heavy boat traffic—the Châtellerault bridge has three arches, the centre spanning just over 160 feet (48 metres). In 1904 the Isar River Bridge at Grünewald, Germany, designed by Emil Morsch for Wayss's firm, became the longest reinforced-concrete span in the world at 230 feet (69 metres).

The longest-spanning concrete arches of the 1920s were designed by the French engineer Eugène Freyssinet. In his bridge over the Seine at Saint-Pierre-du-Vauvray (1922), two thin, hollow arches rise 82 feet (25 metres) at mid-span and are connected by nine crossbeams. The arches curve over the deck, which is suspended by thin steel wires lightly coated with mortar and hanging down in a triangular formation. The 435-foot (131-metre) span, then a record for reinforced concrete, thus has a light appearance. The bridge was destroyed during World War II but was rebuilt in 1946 using the same form.

In 1930 Freyssinet completed his most renowned work, the Plougastel Bridge over the Elorn Estuary near Brest, France. This bridge featured three 585-foot (176-metre) hollow-box arch spans, then the longest concrete spans in the world. Because of the great scale of this structure, Freyssinet studied the creep, or movement under stress, of concrete. This led him to his general idea for prestressing.

In 1943 the Plougastel was eclipsed in length by the Sandö Bridge over the Ångerman River in Sweden. The Sandö Bridge is a thin, single-ribbed, reinforced-concrete arch with a span of 866 feet (260 metres), rising 131 feet (39 metres) above the river.

MAILLART'S INNOVATIONS

Swiss engineer Robert Maillart's use of reinforced concrete, beginning in 1901, effected a revolution in structural art. Maillart, all of whose main bridges are in Switzerland, was the first 20th-century designer to break completely with the masonry tradition and put concrete into forms technically appropriate to its properties yet visually surprising. For his 1901 bridge over the Inn River at Zuoz, he designed a curved arch and a flat roadway connected by longitudinal walls that turned the complete structure into a hollow-box girder with a span of 125 feet (37.5 metres) and with hinges at the abutments and the crown. This was the first concrete hollow-box to be constructed. The arch at Zuoz is thickened at the bottom, and all of the load to the abutments is carried at these thick points. The walls near the abutments, therefore, are technically superfluous. For his 1905 bridge over the Vorderrhein at Tavanasa, with a span of 167 feet (50 metres), Maillart cut out the spandrel walls to achieve a technically superior form that was also visually new. As at Zuoz, the concrete arches of the Tavanasa bridge were connected by hinges to both abutments and to each other at the crown, thus allowing the arch to rise freely without internal stress when the temperature rose and to drop when the temperature went down. By contrast, Hennebique's bridge at Châtellerault did not have hinges, and the arches cracked severely at the abutments and crown. The Tavanasa bridge was unfortunately destroyed by an avalanche in 1927.

Maillart's Valtschielbach Bridge of 1926, a deck-stiffened arch with a 142-foot (43-metre) span, demonstrated that the arch can be extremely thin as long as the deck beam is stiff. The arch at Valtschielbach increases in thickness from a mere 9 inches (23 cm) at the crown to just over 11 inches (28 cm) at the supports. Thin vertical slabs, or cross-walls, connect the arch to the deck, allowing the deck to stiffen the arch and thus permitting the arch to be thin. Such technical insight revealed Maillart's deep understanding of how to work with reinforced concrete—an understanding that culminated in a series of masterpieces beginning with the 1930 Salginatobel Bridge, which, as with the others already mentioned, is located in the Swiss canton of Graubünden. The form of the Salginatobel Bridge is similar to the Tavanasa yet modified to account for a longer central span of 295 feet (89 metres), which is needed to cross the deep ravine below. Maillart's hollow-box, three-hinged arch design not only was the least costly of the 19 designs proposed but also was considered by the district engineer to be the most elegant. The stone abutments of earlier Maillart bridges were dispensed with at Salginatobel, as the rocky walls of the ravine that meet the arch are sufficient to carry the load.

Other notable bridges by Maillart are the bridge over the Thur at Felsegg (1933), the Schwandbach Bridge near

Hinterfultigen (1933), and the Töss River footbridge near Wulflingen (1934). The Felsegg bridge has a 226-foot (68-metre) span and features for the first time two parallel arches, both three-hinged. Like the Salginatobel Bridge, the Felsegg bridge features X-shaped abutment hinges of reinforced concrete (invented by Freyssinet), which were more economical than steel hinges. The Schwandbach Bridge, with a span of 123 feet (37 metres), is a deck-stiffened arch with a horizontally curved roadway. The true character of reinforced concrete is most apparent in this bridge, as the inner edge of the slab-arch follows the horizontal curve of the highway, while the outer edge of the arch is straight. Vertical trapezoidal cross-walls integrate the deck with the arch, and the result is one of the most acclaimed bridges in concrete. The Töss footbridge is a deck-stiffened arch with a span of 125 feet (37.5 metres). The deck is curved vertically at the crown and counter-curved at the riverbanks, integrating the structure into the setting.

Maillart's great contribution to bridge design was that, while he kept within the traditional discipline of engineering, always striving to use less material and keep costs down, he continually played with the forms in order to achieve maximum aesthetic expression. Some of his last bridges — at Vessy, Liesberg, and Lachen — illustrate his mature vision for the possibilities of structural art. Over the Arve River at Vessy in 1935, Maillart designed a three-hinged, hollow-box arch in which the thin cross-walls taper at mid-height, forming an X shape. This striking design, giving life to the structure, is both a natural form and a playful expression. Also in 1935, a beam bridge over the Birs River at Liesberg employed haunching of the beams, a tapering outward at the base of the thin columns, and a curved top edge becoming less deep near the abutments. For a skewed railway overpass at Lachen in 1940, Maillart used two separate three-hinged arches that sprang from different levels of the abutment, creating a dynamic interplay of shapes.

PRESTRESSED CONCRETE

A great innovation in masonry construction arrived with the use of prestressed concrete. Prestressing is achieved by either pretensioning or posttensioning processes. In pretensioning, lengths of steel wire, cables, or ropes are laid in the empty mold and then stretched and anchored. After the concrete has been poured and allowed to set, the anchors are released and, as the steel seeks to return to its original length, it compresses the concrete. In the posttensioning process, the steel is run through ducts formed in the concrete. When the concrete has hardened, the steel is anchored to the exterior of the member by some sort of gripping device. Prestressed concrete neutralizes the stretching forces that would rupture ordinary concrete by compressing an area to the point at which no tension is experienced until the strength of the compressed section is overcome. Because it achieves strength without using heavy steel reinforcements, it has been used to great effect to build lighter, shallower, and more elegant structures such as bridges and vast roofs.

EUGÈNE FREYSSINET

The idea of prestressing concrete was first applied by Freyssinet in his effort to save the Le Veurdre Bridge over the Allier River near Vichy, France. A year after its completion in 1910, Freyssinet noted the three-arch bridge had been moving downward at an alarming rate. A flat concrete arch, under its own dead load, generates huge compressive forces that cause the structure to shorten over time and, hence, move eventually downward.

This "creep" may eventually cause the arch to collapse. Freyssinet's solution was to jack apart the arch halves at the crown, lifting the arch and putting the concrete into additional compression against the abutments and then casting new concrete into the spaces at the crown. By 1928, experience with the Le Veurdre Bridge led Freyssinet to propose the more common method of prestressing, using high-strength steel to put concrete into compression.

Freyssinet's major prestressed works came after the reinforced-concrete Plougastel Bridge and included a series of bridges over the Marne River following World War II. The Luzancy Bridge (1946), with a span of 180 feet (54 metres), demonstrates the lightness and beauty that can be achieved using prestressed concrete for a single-span beam bridge.

The first major bridge made of prestressed concrete in the United States, the Walnut Lane Bridge (1950) in Philadelphia, was designed by Gustave Magnel and features three simply supported girder spans with a centre span of 160 feet (48 metres) and two end spans of 74 feet (22 metres). Although it was plain in appearance, a local art jury responsible for final approval found that the slim lines of the bridge were elegant enough not to require a stone facade.

ULRICH FINSTERWALDER

During the years after World War II, a German engineer and builder, Ulrich Finsterwalder, developed the cantilever method of construction with prestressed concrete. Finsterwalder's Bendorf Bridge over the Rhine at Koblenz, Germany, was completed in 1962 with thin piers and a centre span of 673 feet (202 metres). The double cantilevering method saved money through the absence of scaffolding in the water and also by allowing for reduced girder depth and consequent reduction of material where the ends of the deck meet in the centre. The resulting girder has the appearance of a very shallow arch, elegant in profile. Another fine bridge by Finsterwalder is the Mangfall Bridge (1959) south of Munich, a high bridge with a central span of 354 feet (106 metres) and two side spans of 295 feet (89 metres). The Mangfall Bridge features the first latticed truss walls made of prestressed concrete, and it also has a two-tier deck allowing pedestrians to walk below the roadway and take in a spectacular view of the valley. Finsterwalder successfully sought to show that prestressed concrete could compete directly with steel not only in cost but also in reduction of depth.

CHRISTIAN MENN

The technical and aesthetic possibilities of prestressed concrete were most fully realized in Switzerland with the bridges of Christian Menn. Menn's early arch bridges were influenced by Maillart, but, with prestressing, he was able to build longer-spanning bridges and use new forms. The Reichenau Bridge (1964) over the Rhine, a deck-stiffened arch with a span of 328 feet (98 metres), shows Menn's characteristic use of a wide, prestressed concrete deck slab cantilevering laterally from both sides of a single box. For the high, curving Felsenau Viaduct (1974) over the Aare River in Bern, spans of up to 512 feet (154 metres) were built using the cantilever method from double piers. The trapezoidal box girder, only 36 feet (11 metres) wide at the top, haunches at the supports and carries an 85-foot- (26-metre-) wide turnpike. More impressive yet is the high, curving Ganter Bridge (1980), crossing a deep valley in the canton of Valais. The Ganter is both a cable-stayed and a prestressed cantilever girder bridge, with the highest column rising 492 feet (148 metres) and with a central span of

571 feet (171 metres). The form is unique: the cable-stays are flat and covered by thin concrete slabs, making the bridge look very much like a Maillart bridge upside-down.

STEEL AFTER 1931

With the properties and construction possibilities of steel fully understood in the early 20th century, the way was opened for bridges of greater and greater length.

LONG-SPAN SUSPENSION BRIDGES

The success of the George Washington Bridge—especially its extremely small ratio of girder depth to span—had a great influence on suspension bridge design in the 1930s. Its revolutionary design led to the building of several major bridges, such as the Golden Gate (1937), the Deer Isle (1939), and the Bronx-Whitestone (1939). The Golden Gate Bridge, built over the entrance to San Francisco Bay under the direction of Joseph Strauss, was upon its completion the world's longest span at 4,200 feet (1,260 metres); its towers rise 746 feet (224 metres) above the water. Deer Isle Bridge in Maine, U.S., was designed by David Steinman with only plate girders to stiffen the deck, which was 25 feet (7.5 metres) wide yet had a central span of 1,080 feet (324 metres). Likewise, the deck for Othmar Ammann's Bronx-Whitestone Bridge in New York was originally stiffened only by plate girders; its span reached 2,300 feet (690 metres). Both the Deer Isle and the Bronx-Whitestone bridges later oscillated in wind and had to be modified following the Tacoma Narrows disaster.

TACOMA NARROWS

In 1940 the first Tacoma Narrows Bridge opened over Puget Sound in Washington state, U.S. Spanning 2,800 feet (840 metres), its deck, also stiffened by plate girders, had a depth of only 8 feet (2.4 metres). This gave it a ratio of girder depth to span of 1:350, identical to that of the George Washington Bridge. Unfortunately, at Tacoma Narrows, just four months after the bridge's completion, the deck tore apart and collapsed under a moderate wind. At that time bridges normally were designed to withstand gales of 120 miles (190 km) per hour, yet the wind at Tacoma was only 42 miles (67 km) per hour. Motion pictures taken of the disaster show the deck rolling up and down and twisting wildly. These two motions, vertical and torsional, occurred because the deck had been provided with little vertical and almost no torsional stiffness. Engineers had overlooked the wind-induced failures of bridges in the 19th century and had designed extremely thin decks without fully understanding their aerodynamic behaviour. After the Tacoma bridge failed, however, engineers added trusses to the Bronx-Whitestone bridge, cable-stays to Deer Isle, and further bracing to the stiffening truss at Golden Gate. In turn, the diagonal stays used to strengthen the Deer Isle Bridge led engineer Norman Sollenberger to design the San Marcos Bridge (1951) in El Salvador with inclined suspenders, thus forming a cable truss between cables and deck—the first of its kind.

LESSONS OF THE DISASTER

The disaster at Tacoma caused engineers to rethink their concepts of the vertical motion of suspension bridge decks under horizontal wind loads. Part of the problem at Tacoma was the construction of a plate girder with solid steel plates, 8 feet (2.4 metres) deep on each side, through which the wind could not pass. For this reason, the new Tacoma Narrows Bridge (1950), as well as Ammann's 4,260-foot- (1,280-metre-) span Verrazano Narrows Bridge in New York (1964), were built with open trusses for the deck in order to allow wind passage. The 3,800-foot- (1,140-metre-) span Mackinac Bridge in Michigan, U.S., designed by Steinman, also used a deep truss; its two side spans of 1,800 feet (540 metres) made it the longest continuous suspended structure in the world at the time of its completion in 1957.

The 3,240-foot- (972-metre-) span Severn Bridge (1966), linking southern England and Wales over the Severn River, uses a shallow steel box for its deck, but the deck is shaped aerodynamically in order to allow wind to pass over and under it—much as a cutwater allows water to deflect around piers with a greatly reduced force. Another innovation of the Severn Bridge was the use of steel suspenders from cables to deck that form a series of Vs in profile. When a bridge starts to oscillate in heavy wind, it tends to move longitudinally as well as up and down, and the inclined suspenders of the Severn Bridge act to dampen the longitudinal movement. The design ideas used on the Severn Bridge were repeated on the Bosporus Bridge (1973) at Istanbul and on the Humber Bridge (1981) over the Humber River in England. The Humber Bridge in its turn became the longest-spanning bridge in the world, with a main span of 4,626 feet (1,388 metres).

TRUSS BRIDGES

Although trusses are used mostly as secondary elements in arch, suspension, or cantilever designs, several important simply supported truss bridges have achieved significant length. The Astoria Bridge (1966) over the Columbia River in Oregon, U.S., is a continuous three-span steel truss with a centre span of 1,232 feet (370 metres), and the Tenmon Bridge (1966) at Kumamoto, Japan, has a centre span of 984 feet (295 metres).

In 1977 the New River Gorge Bridge, the world's longest-spanning steel arch, was completed in Fayette County, West Virginia, U.S. Designed by Michael Baker, the two-hinged arch truss carries four lanes of traffic 876 feet (263 metres) above the river and has a span of 1,700 feet (510 metres).

CABLE-STAYED BRIDGES

Beginning in the 1950s, with the growing acceptance of cable-stayed bridges, there came into being a type of structure that could not easily be classified by construction material. Cable-stayed bridges offered a variety of possibilities to the designer regarding not only the materials for deck and cables but also the geometric arrangement of the cables.

GERMAN DESIGNS

Early examples of cable-stayed bridges, such as the Strömsund Bridge in Sweden (1956), used just two cables fastened at nearly the same point high on the tower and fanning out to support the deck at widely separated points. By contrast, the Oberkasseler Bridge, built over the Rhine River in Düsseldorf, Germany, in 1973, used a single tower in the middle of its twin 846-foot (254-metre) spans; the four cables were placed in a harp or parallel arrangement, being equally spaced both up the tower and along the centre line of the deck. The Bonn-Nord Bridge in Bonn, Germany (1966), was the first major cable-stayed bridge to use a large number of thinner cables instead of relatively few but heavier ones—the technical advantage being that, with more cables, a thinner deck might be used. Such multicable arrangements subsequently became quite common. The box girder deck of the Bonn-Nord, as with most cable-stayed bridges built during the 1950s and

'60s, was made of steel. From the 1970s, however, concrete decks were used more frequently.

U.S. DESIGNS

Cable-stayed bridges in the United States reflected trends in both cable arrangement and deck material. The Pasco-Kennewick Bridge (1978) over the Columbia River in Washington state supported its centre span of 981 feet (294 metres) from two double concrete towers, the cables fanning down to the concrete deck on either side of the roadway. Designed by Arvid Grant in collaboration with the German firm of Leonhardt and Andra, its cost was not significantly different from those of other proposals with more conventional designs. The same designers produced the East End Bridge across the Ohio River between Proctorville, Ohio, and Huntington, West Virginia, in 1985. The East End has a major span of 900 feet (270 metres) and a minor span of 608 feet (182 metres). The single concrete tower is shaped like a long triangle in the traverse direction, and the cable arrangement is of the fan type; but, while the Pasco-Kennewick Bridge has two parallel sets of cables, the East End has but one set, fanning out from a single plane at the tower into two planes at the composite steel and concrete deck so that, as one moves from pure profile to a longitudinal view, the cables do not align visually.

The Sunshine Skyway Bridge (1987), designed by Eugene Figg and Jean Mueller over Tampa Bay in Florida, has a main prestressed-concrete span of 1,200 feet (360 metres). It, too, employs a single plane of cables, but these remain in one plane that fans out down the centre of the deck. Another prominent design in cable-stayed bridges in the United States is Dames Point Bridge (1987), designed by Howard Needles in consultation with Ulrich Finsterwalder and crossing the St. Johns River in

Jacksonville, Florida. The main span at Dames Point is 1,300 feet (390 metres), with side spans of 660 feet (200 metres). From H-shaped towers of reinforced concrete, two planes of stays in harp formation support reinforced-concrete girders. The towers are carefully shaped to avoid a stiff appearance.

JAPANESE LONG-SPAN BRIDGES

In the 1970s the Japanese, working primarily with steel, began to build a series of long-span bridges using several forms that by the turn of the 21st century included many of the world's longest spans.

ŌSAKA HARBOUR

In 1974 the Minato Bridge, linking the city of Ōsaka with neighbouring Amagasaki, became one of the world's longest-spanning cantilever truss bridges, at 1,673 feet (502 metres). In 1989 two other impressive and innovative bridges were completed for the purpose of carrying major highways over the port facilities of Ōsaka Harbour. The Konohana suspension bridge carries a four-lane highway on a slender, steel box-beam deck only 10 feet (3 metres) deep. The bridge is self-anchored—that is, the deck has been put into horizontal compression, like that on a cable-stayed bridge, so that there is no force of horizontal tension pulling from the ground at the anchorages. Spanning 984 feet (295 metres), it is the first major suspension bridge to use a single cable. The towers are delta-shaped, with diagonal suspenders running from the cable down the centre of the deck. On the same road as the Konohana is the Ajigawa cable-stayed bridge, with a span of 1,148 feet (344 metres) and an elegantly thin deck just over 10 feet (3 metres) deep.

ISLAND BRIDGES

The Kanmon Bridge (1975), linking the islands of Honshu and Kyushu over the Shimonoseki Strait, was the first major island bridge in Japan. At about this time the Honshu-Shikoku Bridge Authority was formed to connect these two main islands with three lines of bridges and highways. Completed in 1999, the Honshu-Shikoku project was the largest in history, building 6 of the 20 largest spanning bridges in the world as well as the first major set of suspension bridges to carry railroad traffic since John Roebling's Niagara Bridge. The Authority conducted most of the design work itself; unlike projects in other countries, it is not usually possible to identify individual designers for Japanese bridges.

The first part of the project, completed in 1988, is a route connecting the city of Kojima, on the main island of Honshu, to Sakaide, on the island of Shikoku. The Kojima-Sakaide route has three major bridge elements, often referred to collectively as the Seto Ōhashi ("Seto Great Bridge"): the Shimotsui suspension bridge, with a suspended main span of 3,100 feet (940 metres) and two unsuspended side spans of 760 feet (230 metres); the twin 1,380-foot- (420-metre-) span cable-stayed Hitsuishijima and Iwakurojima bridges; and the two nearly identical Bisan-Seto suspension bridges, with main spans of 3,250 feet (990 metres) and 3,610 feet (1,100 metres). The striking towers of the cable-stayed Hitsuishijima and Iwakurojima bridges were designed to evoke symbolic images from Japanese culture, such as the ancient Japanese helmet. The side spans of the two Seto bridges, being fully suspended, give a visual unity to these bridges that is missing from the Shimotsui bridge, where the side spans are supported from below. The double deck of the entire bridge system is a strong 43-foot- (13-metre-) deep continuous truss that carries cars and trucks on the top deck and trains on the lower deck.

The Kojima-Sakaide route forms the middle of the three Honshu-Shikoku links. The eastern route, between Kōbe (Honshu) and Naruto (Shikoku), has only two bridges: the 1985 Ohnaruto suspension bridge and the 1998 Akashi Kaikyō (Akashi Strait) suspension bridge. The Akashi Kaikyō Bridge, now the world's longest suspension bridge, crosses the strait with a main span of 6,530 feet (1,991 metres) and side spans of 3,150 feet (960 metres). Its two 975-foot (297-metre) towers, made of two hollow steel shafts in cruciform section connected by X-bracing, are the tallest bridge towers in the world. The two suspension cables are made of a high-strength steel developed by Japanese engineers for the project. In January 1995 an earthquake that devastated Kōbe had its epicentre almost directly beneath the nearly completed Akashi Kaikyō structure; the bridge survived undamaged, though one tower shifted enough to lengthen the main span by almost one metre.

The western Honshu-Shikoku route links Onomichi (Honshu) with Imabari (Shikoku). One of the major structures is the Ikuchi cable-stayed bridge, with a main span of 1,610 feet (490 metres). The two towers of the Ikuchi Bridge are delta-shaped, with two inclined planes of fan-arranged stays. Also on the Onomichi-Imabari route is the 1979 Ohmishima steel arch bridge, whose 975-foot (297-metre) span made it the longest such structure in the Eastern Hemisphere. But the single most significant structure on the route is the 1999 Tatara cable-stayed bridge, whose main span is 2,920 feet (890 metres). The twin towers of the Tatara Bridge, 720 feet (220 metres) high, have elegant diamond shapes for the lower 459 feet (140 metres); the upper 262 feet (80 metres) consist of two parallel linked shafts that contain the cables.

THE AKASHI STRAIT BRIDGE

Also known to the Japanese as the Pearl Bridge, this structure across the Akashi Strait (Akashi-kaikyo) in west-central Japan became the world's longest suspension bridge when it opened on April 5, 1998. The six-lane road bridge connects the city of Kōbe, on the main island of Honshu, to Iwaya, on Awaji Island, which in turn is linked (via the Ōnaruto Bridge over the Naruto Strait) to the island of Shikoku to the southwest. These two bridges—together with the Seto Great Bridge between Kojima (Honshu) and Sakaide (Shikoku)—are the main components of the Honshu-Shikoku Bridge Project across Japan's Inland Sea.

The three spans of the Akashi Strait Bridge are a total of 12,831 feet (3,911 metres) long. The central span was originally designed to be 6,529 feet (1,990 metres) long, but the Kōbe earthquake of 1995 forced the two towers, which were still under construction, more than 3 feet (about 1 metre) farther apart.

The Akashi Strait Bridge stands in a seismically unstable region that also experiences some of Earth's most severe storms. The bridge engineers used a complex system of counterweights, pendulums, and steel-truss girders to allow the bridge to withstand winds of up to 180 miles (290 km) per hour. Despite these buffers, the bridge can expand and contract as much as 6.5 feet (2 metres) in a single day. The challenges posed by the bridge inspired innovations in wind-tunnel and cable-fabrication technology.

Although railroads have spread around the world, they had their beginning in the work of a small number of engineers of the late 18th and early 19th centuries on both sides of the Atlantic Ocean. The most prominent of those individuals are presented below.

GREAT BRITAIN

The great innovations of the Industrial Revolution are usually traced to Great Britain. The harnessing of the steam engine to a rolling carriage is no exception; the English engineers Richard Trevithick and George Stephenson created two of the first working locomotives.

RICHARD TREVITHICK

English mechanical engineer and inventor Richard Trevithick successfully harnessed high-pressure steam and constructed the world's first steam railway locomotive (1803). In 1805 he adapted his high-pressure engine to driving an iron-rolling mill and to propelling a barge with the aid of paddle wheels.

Trevithick was born on April 13, 1771, in Illogan, Cornwall. He spent his youth at Illogan in the tin-mining district of Cornwall and attended the village school. The schoolmaster described him as "disobedient, slow and obstinate." His father, a mine manager, considered him a loafer, and throughout his career Trevithick remained scarcely literate. Early in life, however, he displayed an extraordinary talent in engineering. Because of his intuitive ability to solve problems that perplexed educated engineers, he obtained his first job as engineer to several Cornish ore mines in 1790 at the age of 19. In 1797 he married Jane Harvey of a prominent engineering family. She bore him six children, one of whom, Francis, became locomotive superintendent of the London & North Western Railway and later wrote a biography of his father.

Because Cornwall has no coalfields, high import costs obliged the ore-mine operators to exercise rigid economy in the consumption of fuel for pumping and hoisting. Cornish engineers, therefore, found it imperative to improve the efficiency of the steam engine. The massive engine then in use was the low-pressure type invented by James Watt. Inventive but cautious, Watt thought that "strong steam" was too dangerous to harness; Trevithick thought differently. He soon realized that, by using high-pressure steam and allowing it to expand within the cylinder, a much smaller and lighter engine could be built without any less power than in the low-pressure type.

Richard Trevithick, detail of an oil painting by John Linnell, 1816; in the Science Museum, London. Courtesy of the Science Museum, London, the Woodcroft Bequest

In 1797 Trevithick constructed high-pressure working models of both stationary and locomotive engines that were so successful that he built a full-scale, high-pressure engine for hoisting ore. In all, he built 30 such engines; they were so compact that they could be transported in an ordinary farm wagon to the Cornish mines, where they were known as "puffer whims" because they vented their steam into the atmosphere.

Trevithick built his first steam carriage, which he drove up a hill in Camborne, Cornwall, on Christmas Eve 1801. The following March, with his cousin Andrew Vivian, he took out his historic patent for high-pressure engines for stationary and locomotive use. In 1803 he built a second carriage, which he drove through the streets of London, and constructed the world's first steam railway locomotive at Samuel Homfray's Penydaren Ironworks in South Wales. On Feb. 21, 1804, that engine won a wager for Homfray by hauling a load of 10 tons of iron and 70 men along 10 miles (16 km) of tramway. A second, similar locomotive was built at Gateshead in 1805, and in 1808 Trevithick demonstrated a third, the *Catch-me-who-can,* on a circular track laid near Euston Road in London. He then abandoned these projects, because the cast-iron rails proved too brittle for the weight of his engines.

In 1805 Trevithick adapted his high-pressure engine to driving an iron-rolling mill and propelling a barge with the aid of paddle wheels. His engine also powered the world's first steam dredgers (1806) and drove a threshing machine on a farm (1812). Such engines could not have succeeded without the improvements Trevithick made in the design and construction of boilers. For his small engines, he built a boiler and engine as a single unit, but he also designed a large wrought-iron boiler with a single internal flue, which became known throughout the world as the Cornish type. It was used in conjunction with the equally famous Cornish pumping engine, which Trevithick perfected with the aid of local engineers. The latter was twice as economic as the Watt type, which it rapidly replaced.

Trevithick, a quick-tempered and impulsive man, was entirely lacking in business sense. An untrustworthy partner caused the failure of a London business he started in 1808 for the manufacture of a type of iron tank Trevithick had patented; bankruptcy followed in 1811. Three years later, nine of Trevithick's engines were ordered for the Peruvian silver mines, and, dreaming of unlimited mineral wealth in the Andes Mountains, he sailed to South America in 1816. After many adventures, he returned to England in 1827, penniless, to find that in his absence other engineers, notably George Stephenson, had profited from his inventions. He died in poverty on April 22, 1833, in Dartford, Kent, and was buried in an unmarked grave.

GEORGE STEPHENSON

English engineer George Stephenson was the principal inventor of the railroad locomotive.

Stephenson was born on June 9, 1781, in Wylam, Northumberland. He was the son of a mechanic who operated a Newcomen atmospheric-steam engine that was used to pump out a coal mine at Newcastle upon Tyne. The boy went to work at an early age and without formal schooling; by age 19 he was operating a Newcomen engine. His curiosity aroused by the Napoleonic war news, he enrolled in night school and learned to read and write. He soon married and, in order to earn extra income, learned to repair shoes, fix clocks, and cut clothes for miners' wives, getting a mechanic friend, the future Sir William Fairbairn, to take over his engine part-time. His genius with steam engines, however, presently won him the post of engine wright (chief mechanic) at Killingworth colliery.

Stephenson's first wife died, leaving him with a young son, Robert, whom he sent to a Newcastle school to learn mathematics; every night when the boy came home, father and son went over the homework together, both learning. In 1813 George Stephenson visited a neighbouring colliery to examine a "steam boiler on wheels" constructed by John Blenkinsop to haul coal out of the mines. In the belief that the heavy contraption could not gain traction on smooth wooden rails, Blenkinsop had given it a ratchet wheel running on a cogged third rail, an arrangement that created frequent breakdowns. Stephenson thought he could do better, and, after conferring with Lord Ravensworth, the principal owner of Killingworth, he built the *Blucher*, an engine that drew eight loaded wagons carrying 30 tons of coal at 4 miles (6 km) per hour. Not satisfied, he sought to improve his locomotive's power and introduced the "steam blast," by which exhaust steam was redirected up the chimney, pulling air after it and increasing the draft. The new design made the locomotive truly practical.

Over the next few years, Stephenson built several locomotives for Killingworth and other collieries and gained a measure of fame by inventing a mine-safety lamp. In 1821 he heard of a project for a railroad, employing draft horses, to be built from Stockton to Darlington to facilitate exploitation of a rich vein of coal. At Darlington he interviewed the promoter, Edward Pease, and so impressed him that Pease commissioned him to build a steam locomotive for the line. On Sept. 27, 1825, railroad transportation was born when the first public passenger train, pulled by Stephenson's *Active* (later renamed *Locomotion*), ran from Darlington to Stockton, carrying 450 persons at 15 miles (24 km) per hour. Liverpool and Manchester interests called him in to build a 40-mile (64-km) railroad line to connect the two cities. To survey and construct the line, Stephenson had to outwit the violent hostility of farmers and landlords who feared, among other things, that the railroad would supplant horse-drawn transportation and shut off the market for oats.

When the Liverpool-Manchester line was nearing completion in 1829, a competition was held for locomotives; Stephenson's new engine, the *Rocket*, which he built with his son, Robert, won with a speed of 36 miles (58 km) per hour. Eight locomotives were used when the Liverpool-Manchester line opened on Sept. 15, 1830, and all of them had been built in Stephenson's Newcastle works. From this time on, railroad building spread rapidly throughout Britain, Europe, and North America, and George Stephenson continued as the chief guide of the revolutionary transportation medium, solving problems of roadway construction, bridge design, and locomotive and rolling-stock manufacture. He built many other railways in the Midlands, and he acted as consultant on many railroad projects at home and abroad. He died on Aug. 12, 1848, in Chesterfield, Derbyshire.

THE UNITED STATES

The other great English-speaking centre of the Industrial Revolution, the United States, was not idle while Great Britain was industrious. In America, too, innovations came out of the work of inventors and engineers such as Oliver Evans, Peter Cooper, and John Jervis.

OLIVER EVANS

American inventor Oliver Evans pioneered the high-pressure steam engine (U.S. patent, 1790) and created the first continuous production line (1784).

Evans was born on Sept. 13, 1755, near Newport, Del. He was apprenticed to a wheelwright at the age of 16.

Observing the trick of a blacksmith's boy who used the propellant force of steam in a gun, he began to investigate ways to harness steam for propulsion. Before he could successfully pursue this line of research, however, he became involved with a number of other industrial problems. Carding, or combing, fibres to prepare them for spinning was a laborious process constituting a bottleneck in the newly mechanized production of textiles. To speed this operation Evans invented a machine that cut and mounted 1,000 wire teeth per minute on leather, the teeth serving as an improved carding device.

In 1784, at the age of 29, he attacked another major industrial production problem, the age-old process of grinding grain. Building a factory outside Philadelphia and adapting five machines, including conveyors, elevators, and weighing scales, he created a production line in which all movement throughout the mill was automatic. Labour was required only to set the mill in motion; power was supplied by waterwheels, and grain was fed in at one end, passed by a system of conveyors and chutes through the stages of milling and refining, and emerged at the other end as finished flour. The system, which reduced costs by 50 percent according to Evans' calculations, much later was widely copied in American flour milling.

When Evans applied for patent protection, first to state governments (1787) and later to the new U.S. Patent Office (1790), he added a third invention, his high-pressure steam engine. He continued to work on this for the next several years, envisioning both a stationary engine for industrial purposes and an engine for land and water transport. In 1801 he built in Philadelphia a stationary engine that turned a rotary crusher to produce pulverized limestone for agricultural purposes. The engine that became associated with his name was an original adaptation of the existing steam engine; Evans placed both the cylinder and the crankshaft at the same end of the beam instead of at opposite ends, as had been done previously. This greatly reduced the weight of the beam. An ingenious linkage, which became world famous as the Evans straight-line linkage, made the new arrangement feasible. He saw at once the potential of such an engine for road transportation but was unable to persuade the authorities to permit its use on the Pennsylvania Turnpike—not unnaturally, since it might well have frightened the horses, which at that time provided the main form of transport. Within a few years he had engines doing several other kinds of work, including sowing grain, driving sawmills and boring machines, and powering a dredge to clear the Philadelphia water frontage. Completed by June 1805, his new type of steam-engine scow, called the Orukter Amphibolos, or Amphibious Digger, was 30 feet (9 metres) long by 12 feet (3.7 metres) wide. In its machinery it embodied the chain-of-buckets principle of his automatic flour mill. Equipped with wheels, it ran on land as well as on water, making it the first powered road vehicle to operate in the United States.

In 1806 Evans began to develop his noted Mars Iron Works, where, over the next 10 years, he made more than 100 steam engines that were used with screw presses for processing cotton, tobacco, and paper. The Navy Yard in Washington, D.C., bought one of Evans' engines, and, when the War of 1812 broke out, Evans and a partner proposed to build a powerful steam warship with a large gun at the bow, thus anticipating John Ericsson's *Monitor* of 50 years later; but the proposal was not accepted.

Evans' last great work, completed in 1817, was a 24-horsepower high-pressure engine for a waterworks. He died on April 15, 1819, in New York, shortly after a disastrous fire that destroyed his Mars Iron Works, including his valuable patterns and molds.

His *Young Mill-Wright and Miller's Guide,* which he had written in 1792, continued to sell and had gone through 15 editions by 1860. In another work, *The Abortion of the Young Steam Engineer's Guide* (1805), he forecast the need for government subsidization of technological advances.

Vested interests in horses, as well as poor roads, steep gradients, inadequate springing, and an inadequate technology of materials, hindered the adoption of his ideas for steam engines on roads. Also, because later manufacturers were slow to make use of his innovative manufacturing techniques, Evans was long a somewhat neglected figure. More recently, however, in the allocation of priorities for the development of the high-pressure steam engine, the simultaneity of Evans' work with that of the British genius Richard Trevithick has been established, and historians have accorded proper credit for his pioneering of the assembly line.

PETER COOPER

American inventor, manufacturer, and philanthropist Peter Cooper built the pioneering locomotive *Tom Thumb* and founded the Cooper Union for the Advancement of Science and Art, New York City.

Cooper was born on Feb. 12, 1791, in New York City. Son of a Revolutionary War army officer who went into a succession of businesses in New York, Cooper learned an array of trades at an early age, despite having had only a single year of formal schooling. At the age of 17 he was apprenticed to a coach maker, whom he served so well that he was given a salary, and at the end of his apprenticeship was offered a loan to go into coach making on his own. Young Cooper instead went into the business of manufacturing and selling machines for shearing cloth. A few years later he saw opportunity in another industry and switched to supplying the rapidly growing markets for glue and isinglass, building up a large business that in 1828 he entrusted to his son Edward and his son-in-law Abram S. Hewitt, while he himself plunged into still another enterprise. This was the Canton Iron Works, built on 3,000 acres of land in Baltimore, primarily to supply the new Baltimore and Ohio Railroad Company. The route of the railroad, however, was so hilly and twisting that English engineers despaired of running an engine over it. Cooper at once undertook to build a suitable locomotive and by 1830 had the diminutive but powerful *Tom Thumb* experimentally pulling a load of 40 persons at 10 miles (16 km) per hour.

The resulting success of the B&O contributed to Cooper's rapid expansion of business interests and growing fortune. In 1854, in his new factory at Trenton, N.J., the first structural-iron beams for buildings were rolled. He persevered in his support of Cyrus Field's Atlantic cable project until it was successfully concluded, and he became president of the North American Telegraph Company. During the same period he displayed remarkable inventive talent, producing a washing machine, a compressed-air engine for ferry boats, a waterpower device for moving canal barges, and several other devices.

Cooper's social views were farsighted; as a member of the Board of Aldermen of New York City, he advocated paid police and firemen, public schools, and improved public sanitation. In 1859 he founded Cooper Union, where free courses were offered in science, engineering, and art. In the presidential election of 1876 he headed the minority Greenback Party ticket in order to place before the public his economic views, which ran counter to the prevailing deflationary doctrine. At a reception in his

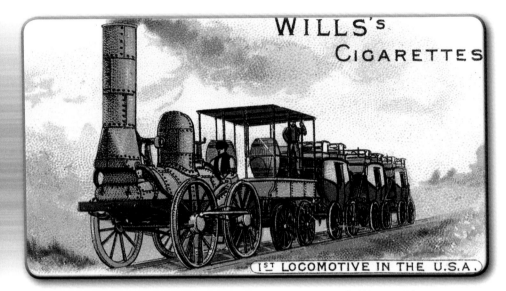

Stourbridge Lion, locomotive designed by John Bloomfield Jervis. Photos. com/Jupiterimages

honour in his later years he summed up his philosophy: "I have endeavoured to remember that the object of life is to do good." Cooper died on April 4, 1883, in New York City.

JOHN JERVIS

American civil engineer John Bloomfield Jervis made outstanding contributions in the construction of U.S. canals, railroads, and water-supply systems.

Jervis was born on Dec. 14, 1795, in Huntington, N.Y. He worked as an axman on the survey for the Erie Canal and earned rapid promotion on that project thereafter, serving as chief engineer from 1821 to 1825. In 1827 he became chief engineer for the Delaware and Hudson Canal project, which was designed to carry coal from Pennsylvania to New York City via the Hudson River. This project consisted of building and linking together a 108-mile (174-km) canal and a 16-mile (26-km) railway, which involved the construction of numerous bridges and inclines in the mountains. Jervis planned and designed every facet of the railway, and he drew up the specifications for its locomotive, the *Stourbridge Lion*, which was the first functioning locomotive in the United States.

Jervis next became chief engineer of the Mohawk & Hudson Railway, New York state's first railroad. In this post he designed the *Experiment* (1832), the first locomotive to have four of its six wheels mounted on a swiveling truck. This radical innovation enabled the *Experiment* to reach speeds of up to 60 miles (100 km) per hour, making it the fastest locomotive in the world.

From 1833 to 1836, Jervis was chief engineer of the Chenango Canal in New York, which was the first canal to use artificial reservoirs as part of its water supply. In 1836 he took charge of construction of the Croton Aqueduct, New York City's first water-supply system, and he directed the construction of the Croton Dam and Reservoir as well as the Aqueduct Bridge, which was built on 15 stone arches and crossed the Harlem River. In 1846 Jervis served as the consulting engineer for the Boston water-supply system.

Jervis returned to railroads in 1847, and over the next 14 years he worked as a consulting or chief engineer for several railroad companies, including the Hudson River Railroad and the Michigan Southern and Northern Indiana Railroad. In 1854 he became president of the Chicago and Rock Island Railway and in 1861 general superintendent of the Pittsburgh, Fort Wayne and Chicago Railway. He died on Jan. 12, 1885, in Rome, N.Y.

CHAPTER 9
RAILROAD TYCOONS OF THE GILDED AGE

The Gilded Age was a period of gross materialism and blatant political corruption in U.S. history that began just after the Civil War ended in 1865. At that time the young nation was finally able to direct its complete attention and its considerable energies west of the Mississippi River. There the vast reaches of prairie and mountain waited to be crossed by rail so that the riches of the Pacific could be brought within view.

No better symbol of post-Civil War corruption can be found than the Crédit Mobilier scandal, an illegal manipulation of contracts by a construction and finance company associated with the building of the Union Pacific Railroad (1865–69). In a wide-open period of U.S. history often referred to as the "Great Barbecue," the operations of the Crédit Mobilier were more or less typical. But sensational newspaper exposures and congressional investigations of the company focused attention on a type of corruption that was understood to lie in the unprincipled attitudes of the wild and lawless West. Even those railroads that were not touched by the scandal were understood to bear a trace of its corruption, in that they, too, were created or manipulated by "robber barons" or tycoons—men of enormous wealth who did not bother to hide it, and of great influence who did not hesitate to use it. Some of these men and their companies are profiled below.

THE ERIE RAILROAD COMPANY

The Erie Railroad ran between New York City, Buffalo, and Chicago, through the southern counties of New York state and skirting Lake Erie. It was incorporated in 1832 as the New York and Erie Railroad Company, to build from Piermont, N.Y., on the west bank of the Hudson River, to Dunkirk on Lake Erie. The track was completed in 1851.

The Erie became known as "the scarlet woman of Wall Street" in the mid-19th century when it was the object of financial struggles between Daniel Drew, Jay Gould, James Fisk, and Cornelius Vanderbilt. Drew became a director of the Erie in 1857 and used his position to manipulate the value of Erie stock to his own advantage. In 1868 Vanderbilt, owner of the New York Central Railroad, tried to gain control of the line by cornering its stock. Drew, in an alliance with Gould and Fisk, manufactured 50,000 shares of Erie stock and dumped them on the market. When a court ordered their arrest, they fled to a hotel in Jersey City. Gould was able to bribe legislators in Albany to secure passage of a bill legalizing what they had done. After making peace with Vanderbilt, Gould and Fisk were left in control of the Erie. They used it as a base for new exploits in stock watering and financial chicanery that led to the panic of 1869.

The Erie went bankrupt four times in its history. It had the disadvantage of competing with other railroads between the Midwest and the East Coast. In the 1870s a fierce rate war took place between the Erie, the Baltimore and Ohio, the Grand Trunk, the New York Central, and the Pennsylvania railroads, ending in bankruptcy for the Erie.

The line passed through a number of reorganizations until it merged with the Delaware, Lackawanna and Western Railroad Company in 1960 to become the Erie

Lackawanna Railway Company. Before merger, the Erie had operated 2,300 miles (3,700 km) of track. The merger eliminated duplicating track, resulting in a 2,900-mile road. Despite this, the Erie Lackawanna became bankrupt in 1972 and in 1976 was taken over by Consolidated Rail Corporation (Conrail), a publicly owned company established by the federal government to take over six bankrupt northeastern railroads.

JAY GOULD

American railroad executive, financier, and speculator Jay Gould was an important railroad developer and also one of the most unscrupulous "robber barons" of 19th-century American capitalism.

Jason Gould was born on May 27, 1836, in Roxbury, N.Y. He was educated in local schools and first worked as a surveyor in New York state. He then operated a tannery, and by 1859 he had begun speculating in the securities of small railways. He continued to deal in railroad stocks in New York City during the American Civil War, and in 1863 he became manager of the Rensselaer and Saratoga Railway. He bought and reorganized the Rutland and Washington Railway, and in 1867 he became a director of the Erie Railroad. In 1868 he joined Daniel Drew and Jim Fisk in a struggle to keep Cornelius Vanderbilt from wresting away their control of this railroad. To this end, Gould engaged in outrageous financial manipulations, including the issue of fraudulent stock and the payment of lavish bribes to New York state legislators to legalize that stock's sale. Gould ended up in control of the railroad, and he and Fisk then joined forces with William "Boss" Tweed and Peter Sweeney to profit from further unscrupulous speculations using Erie stock. The four men's attempt to corner the market in loose gold caused the panic of "Black Friday"

(Sept. 24, 1869), when the price, in paper money, of $100 in gold specie, after being driven up to $163.50 by market bidding, fell to $133 when the U.S. Treasury placed $4 million in specie on the market. The disastrous panic that ensued ruined many investors and led to a public outcry against Gould, who was finally forced to relinquish control of the Erie Railroad in 1872, after Fisk had died and the Tweed Ring in New York City had been broken up.

Now possessed of a fortune of $25 million, Gould turned his attention to railroads in the West. He began buying large blocks of Union Pacific Railroad stock and acquired control of that railway by 1874. He bought other lines as well, so that by 1881, at its peak, his railroad empire was the largest one in the nation, totaling about 15,800 miles (25,500 km) of track, or 15 percent of the United States' total rail mileage. Having made large profits from manipulating the company's stock, Gould pulled out of the Union Pacific by 1882. He began building a new railway system, centred on the Missouri Pacific Railroad, that constituted one-half of all trackage in the Southwest by 1890.

In 1881 Gould gained control of the Western Union Telegraph Company after he had weakened that company with cutthroat competition from his own smaller telegraph companies. Gould also owned the *New York World*

George Jay Gould.
Encyclopædia Britannica, Inc.

newspaper from 1879 to 1883, and by 1886 he had acquired the Manhattan Elevated Railroad, which held a monopoly over New York City's elevated railways.

Gould remained ruthless, unscrupulous, and friendless to the end. He died on Dec. 2, 1892, in New York City, leaving a fortune estimated at $77 million.

George Jay Gould (1864–1923), his eldest son, also became a prominent railway owner and was president of the Missouri Pacific, the Texas and Pacific, and several other railways.

DANIEL DREW

Daniel Drew was an American railway financier of the 19th-century "robber baron" era.

He was born on July 29, 1797, in Carmel, N.Y. After a successful career as a cattle trader, Drew bought an interest in a New York-to-Peekskill steamboat in 1834 and six years later established the People's Line. He also bought control of the Stonington Line on Long Island Sound and operated a steamship service on Lake Champlain. His growing capital enabled him in 1844 to open the Wall Street brokerage firm of Drew, Robinson, and Company, which became one of the principal traders in railroad stocks in the United States.

Drew's association with the Erie Railroad began in 1853. The "Erie War" of 1866–68, in which Drew joined Jay Gould and James Fisk in opposing Cornelius Vanderbilt, who sought to buy control of the Erie Railroad, eventually led to his ruin. In the panic of 1873 his losses were considerable, and in March 1876 he filed for bankruptcy. He died on Sept. 18, 1879, in New York City. An avowed Methodist, Drew had contributed some of his earlier wealth to the founding of Drew Theological Seminary at Madison, N.J., and a smaller women's seminary at his birthplace.

A caricature of James Fisk, c. 1860s. Library of Congress, Washington, D.C.

JAMES FISK

A flamboyant financier known as the "Barnum of Wall Street," James Fisk joined speculator Jay Gould in securities manipulations and railroad raiding.

Fisk was born on April 1, 1834, in Bennington, Vt. He worked successively as a circus hand, waiter, peddler, dry-goods salesman, stockbroker, and corporate official. In 1866 he formed Fisk and Belden, a brokerage firm, with the support of Daniel Drew. The following year Fisk joined Drew and Gould in protecting their control of the Erie Railroad from Cornelius Vanderbilt by issuing fraudulent stock. As vice president and comptroller, Fisk used corporate funds to corrupt public officials, produce Broadway shows, and support Broadway beauties, especially the well-known Josie Mansfield, to such an extent that he was also called "The Prince of the Erie."

With Drew's help, Fisk aided Gould in an attempt to corner the gold market by inflating the price, a venture that brought them vast sums but led to the panic of "Black Friday," Sept. 24, 1869. Because Gould secretly sold much of his gold before prices fell, Fisk lost a considerable part of his investment. The repercussions of their actions were disastrous for the nation's business and were felt even in Europe. In New York City on Jan. 6, 1872, after quarrels over Josie Mansfield and business matters, an associate, Edward Stokes, fatally shot Fisk. Fisk died the following day.

THE NEW YORK CENTRAL RAILROAD COMPANY

The New York Central was one of the major American railroads that connected the East Coast with the interior. Founded in 1853, it was a consolidation of 10 small railroads that paralleled the Erie Canal between Albany and Buffalo; the earliest was the Mohawk and Hudson, New York state's first railway, which opened in 1831.

The New York Central's moving spirit was Erastus Corning (1794–1872), four times mayor of Albany, who for 20 years had been president of the Utica and Schenectady, one of the consolidated roads. He served as president of the New York Central until 1864. In 1867 Cornelius Vanderbilt won control, after beating down the Central's stock, and combined it with his New York and Hudson railroads running from Manhattan to Albany.

Vanderbilt joined the New York Central to the Lake Shore and Michigan Southern Railway in 1873, extending his system from Buffalo to Chicago. He added the Michigan Central in 1871. Under his son William, the Central acquired the New York, West Shore, and Buffalo Railroad on the west side of the Hudson River in 1885. The system grew until it had 10,000 miles (16,000 km) of track linking New York with Boston, Montreal, Chicago, and St. Louis.

After World War II the New York Central began to decline. Between 1946 and 1958 it dropped four of its six fast daily passenger runs between New York and Chicago. Efforts to merge with its chief competitor, the also ailing Pennsylvania Railroad Company, culminated in 1968 with the creation of the Penn Central Transportation Company—a merger that later included the New York, New Haven and Hartford Railroad, in 1969. The new colossus had 21,000 miles (33,600 km) of track. Its creators hoped to achieve a division of labour, sending freight to New York and New England north along the New York Central's water-level route while the Pennsylvania main tracks served the industrial needs of Philadelphia, Baltimore, and the Delaware and Schuylkill valleys.

The merger failed, however, and the new road was forced into bankruptcy in June 1970. Passenger services were taken over by the federally established National Railroad Passenger Corporation (Amtrak) in 1971. The company's other railroad assets were merged with five other lines in Consolidated Rail Corporation (Conrail) in April 1976, although the New York–Washington route was later transferred to Amtrak.

CORNELIUS VANDERBILT

Cornelius Vanderbilt was a shipping and railroad magnate who acquired a personal fortune of more than $100 million.

Vanderbilt was born on May 27, 1794, in Port Richmond, Staten Island, N.Y., the son of an impoverished farmer and boatman. He quit school at age 11 to work on the waterfront. In 1810 he purchased his first boat with money borrowed from his parents. He used the boat to ferry passengers between Staten Island and New York City; then, during the War of 1812, he enlarged his operation to a small fleet with which he supplied government outposts around the city.

Vanderbilt expanded his ferry operation still further following the war, but in 1818 he sold all his boats and went to work for Thomas Gibbons as steamship captain. While in Gibbons' employ (1818–29), Vanderbilt learned the steamship business and acquired the capital that he used in 1829 to start his own steamship company.

During the next decade, Vanderbilt gained control of the traffic on the Hudson River by cutting fares and offering unprecedented luxury on his ships. His hard-pressed competitors finally paid him handsomely in return for Vanderbilt's agreement to move his operation. He then concentrated on the northeastern seaboard, offering transportation from Long Island to Providence and Boston. By 1846 the "Commodore," as he was often called, was a millionaire.

The following year, he formed a company to transport passengers and goods from New York City and New Orleans to San Francisco via Nicaragua. With the enormous demand for passage to the West Coast brought about by the 1849 gold rush, Vanderbilt's Accessory Transit Company proved a huge success. He quit the business only after his competitors—whom he had nearly ruined—agreed to pay him $40,000 (later it rose to $56,000) a month to abandon his operation.

By the 1850s he had turned his attention to railroads, buying up so much stock in the New York and Harlem

Railroad that by 1863 he owned the line. He later acquired the Hudson River Railroad and the New York Central Railroad and consolidated them in 1869. When he added the Lake Shore and Michigan Southern Railroad in 1873, Vanderbilt was able to offer the first rail service from New York City to Chicago.

During the last years of his life, Vanderbilt ordered the construction of Grand Central Terminal in New York City, a project that gave jobs to thousands who had become unemployed during the Panic of 1873. Although never interested in philanthropy while acquiring the bulk of his huge fortune, later in his life he did give $1 million to Central University in Nashville, Tenn. (later Vanderbilt University). He died on Jan. 4, 1877, in New York City. In his will he left $90 million to his son William Henry, $7.5 million to William's four sons, and—consistent with his lifelong contempt for women—the relatively small remainder to his second wife and his eight daughters.

WILLIAM VANDERBILT

William Vanderbilt was a railroad magnate and philanthropist who nearly doubled the Vanderbilt family fortune established and in large part bequeathed to him by his father, Cornelius.

William Henry Vanderbilt was born on May 8, 1821, in New Brunswick, N.J. A frail and seemingly unambitious youth, he was dismissed by his strong and dynamic father as incompetent to run the family business. The two split on William's decision to marry at age 19, and Cornelius sent his son off to farm on Staten Island. To his father's surprise, William made the farm a profitable operation.

While Cornelius was still concentrating on steamship lines, William became interested in railroads. In 1857 he convinced his father to make him receiver of the bankrupt

Staten Island Railroad and a few years later startled his father by putting the line back on a sound financial footing. In 1864 William became vice president of the New York and Harlem Railroad and assumed the same position with the Hudson River Railroad in 1865; both lines were owned by his father.

It was not until after the Commodore's death in 1877 that William was fully able to demonstrate his financial and managerial genius. He greatly expanded the New York Central network and acquired the Chicago and North Western; the Nickel Plate (New York, Chicago, & St. Louis); Cleveland, Columbus, Cincinnati, and Indianapolis; and other railroads. He fought regulation of the railroads as he engaged in rate wars and gave special rates to favoured shippers. By the time poor health forced him to resign his railroad presidencies in 1883, William Henry had nearly doubled the Vanderbilt family fortune.

In addition, he established the Vanderbilt family name in philanthropy. He gave substantial gifts to Vanderbilt University, Columbia's College of Physicians and Surgeons, and other recipients. He built a block-long mansion on Fifth Avenue and filled it with what was claimed to be the finest private collection of paintings and sculpture in the world. He died in New York on Dec. 8, 1885. In his will he divided his fortune more equitably than had his father, and he left substantial bequests to the Metropolitan Museum of Art, the YMCA, and various churches and hospitals.

THE NORTHERN PACIFIC AND GREAT NORTHERN RAILWAYS

The Northern Pacific and the Great Northern were two northern transcontinental railroads of the United States, operating between the upper Midwest and the Pacific

Coast in Washington. They merged into the Burlington Northern in 1970.

The Northern Pacific was chartered by Congress in 1864 to build a line from Lake Superior westward to a port on the Pacific coast and was given a land grant of 40,000,000 acres (16,200,000 hectares). It nevertheless encountered difficulty in finding financial backing for its venture into a mostly unsettled wilderness until the Philadelphia banker Jay Cooke undertook to raise $100 million. In 1873 the railroad was approaching Bismarck, in the Dakota Territory, when Cooke's bank collapsed. The road went into receivership, and construction stopped for six years. In 1878 the railroad was taken over by Henry Villard, who built it westward to Helena in Montana Territory, where it was connected with the Oregon Railway to Seattle in Washington Territory in 1883.

The Northern Pacific encountered new financial difficulties in the 1890s, when it was reorganized by the banker J.P. Morgan. Morgan shared control of it with James J. Hill, whose Great Northern Railway Company was a close competitor. The Great Northern had developed out of a struggling Minnesota railroad, the St. Paul and Pacific Railroad (SP&P), which Hill and three associates had purchased in 1878. Hill was a Minnesota coal and freight merchant who knew the north country well and believed he could build the decaying SP&P into a great railroad. He extended it north to the Canadian border to link up with a Canadian line to Winnipeg, and then westward through the Dakotas and Montana, reaching Great Falls in 1887 and the Pacific coast at Everett, Wash., in 1893. Hill induced thousands of homesteaders, mostly from Scandinavia, to settle along his tracks as he built them westward. In 1890 the system's name was changed to the Great Northern.

To supply cargo for his railroad, Hill developed export markets in the Orient for American cotton, flour, and metals. Eastbound, the road carried lumber from the Pacific Northwest to the midwestern prairies. Together with Morgan, Hill bought control of the Chicago, Burlington & Quincy Railroad Company in 1901. This gave both railroads a link to Chicago, St. Louis, and the cotton-hauling railroads of the South. In the same year, Hill set up the Northern Securities Company, a holding company to control the three railroads, with himself as president. The U.S. Supreme Court declared it in violation of the Sherman Anti-Trust Act in 1904 and ordered the company dissolved. The three railroads continued to be financially linked, however, and in 1970 they were permitted to merge as the Burlington Northern, Inc.

With the addition of the St. Louis–San Francisco Railway Company in 1980, the Burlington system became the largest in the United States, with about 30,000 miles (48,000 km) of track stretching from the West Coast through the Rocky Mountains to the Great Lakes and down to the Gulf of Mexico. In 1995 the Burlington Northern acquired the Santa Fe Pacific Corporation, giving it additional trackage in the south-central and southwestern United States. The company, now known as the Burlington Northern Santa Fe Corporation, is headquartered in Fort Worth, Tex.

JAY COOKE

Jay Cooke was a banker, railroad financier, and fund-raiser for the U.S. government during the American Civil War.

Cooke was born on Aug. 10, 1821, in Sandusky, Ohio. At 18 he entered the Philadelphia banking house of E.W. Clark and Co., and three years later he became a member of the firm. In 1861 he opened his own banking house in Philadelphia and floated a war loan of $3 million for the state of Pennsylvania. He was engaged by the United

States Treasury Department in 1862 for the sale of $500 million worth of bonds. His services were secured again in 1865, when he disposed of three series of notes totaling $830 million. In 1870 Cooke's firm undertook to finance the construction of the Northern Pacific Railway but failed at the approach of the financial crisis of 1873. By 1880 he had discharged all his obligations and had again become wealthy. He died on Feb. 18, 1905, in Ogontz, Pa.

HENRY VILLARD

Henry Villard was a journalist and financier who became one of the major American railroad and electric utility promoters.

Ferdinand Heinrich Gustav Hilgard was born on April 10, 1835, in Speyer, Bavaria. He immigrated to the United States in 1853 and was employed by German-American newspapers and later by leading American dailies. He reported (1858) the Lincoln–Douglas debates for eastern newspapers and the Pikes Peak gold rush (1859) for the *Cincinnati Daily Commercial*. During the Civil War he was a war correspondent, first for the *New York Herald* and then for the *New York Tribune*. In 1881 he purchased *The Nation* and the *New York Evening Post*.

As an agent for German bondholders, Villard became involved in railway organization. In 1875 he helped reorganize the Oregon and California Railroad and the Oregon Steamship Company and the following year became president of both companies. He organized the Oregon Railway and Navigation Company in 1879 and built a railroad along the Columbia River from Portland, Ore., to Wallula, Wash. In 1881 he secured control of the predecessor of the Northern Pacific, of which he became president. Its transcontinental line was completed under his management, but the costs so far exceeded the estimate that financial pressures forced him to resign from the presidency in 1884. He later recouped his losses, and from 1888 to 1893 he served as chairman of the board of directors of the same company. He bought the Edison Lamp Company, Newark, N.J., and the Edison Machine Works, Schenectady, N.Y., and formed them into the Edison General Electric Company in 1889, serving as president until its reorganization in 1893 as the General Electric Company. Villard died on Nov. 12, 1900, in Dobbs Ferry, N.Y.

J.P. MORGAN

Financier and industrial organizer J.P. Morgan was one of the world's foremost financial figures during the two decades before World War I. He reorganized several major railroads and consolidated the United States Steel, International Harvester, and General Electric corporations.

The son of a successful financier, Junius Spencer Morgan (1813–90), John Pierpont Morgan was born on April 17, 1837, in Hartford, Conn. Educated in Boston and at the University of Göttingen, Ger., he began his career in 1857 as an accountant with the New York banking firm of Duncan, Sherman and Company, which was the American representative of the London firm George Peabody and Company. In 1861 Morgan became the agent for his father's banking company in New York City. During 1864–71 he was a member of the firm of Dabney, Morgan and Company, and in 1871 he became a partner in the New York City firm of Drexel, Morgan and Company, which soon became the predominant source of U.S. government financing. This firm was reorganized as J.P. Morgan and Company in 1895, and, largely through Morgan's ability, it became one of the most powerful banking houses in the world.

Because of his links with the Peabody firm, Morgan had intimate and highly useful connections with the London financial world, and during the 1870s he was thereby able to provide the rapidly growing industrial corporations of the United States with much-needed capital from British bankers. He began reorganizing railroads in 1885, when he arranged an agreement between two of the largest railroads in the country, the New York Central Railroad and the Pennsylvania Railroad, that minimized a potentially destructive rate war and rail-line competition between them. In 1886 he reorganized two more major railroads with the aim of stabilizing their financial base. In the course of these corporate restructurings, Morgan became a member of the board of directors of these and other railroads, thereby amassing great influence on them. Between 1885 and 1888 he extended his influence to lines based in Pennsylvania and Ohio, and after the financial panic of 1893 he was called upon to rehabilitate a large number of the leading rail lines in the country, including the Southern Railroad, the Erie Railroad, and the Northern Pacific. He helped to achieve railroad rate stability and discouraged overly chaotic competition in the East. By gaining control of much of the stock of the railroads that he reorganized, he became one of the world's most powerful railroad magnates, controlling about 5,000 miles (8,000 km) of American railroads by 1902.

During the depression that followed the Panic of 1893, Morgan formed a syndicate that resupplied the U.S. government's depleted gold reserve with $62 million in gold in order to relieve a Treasury crisis. Three years later he began financing a series of giant industrial consolidations that were to reshape the corporate structure of the American manufacturing sector. His first venture, in 1891, was to arrange the merger of Edison General Electric and

Thomson-Houston Electric Company to form General Electric, which became the dominant electrical-equipment manufacturing firm in the United States. Having financed the creation of the Federal Steel Company in 1898, Morgan in 1901 joined in merging it with the giant Carnegie Steel Company and other steel companies to form United States Steel Corporation, which was the world's first billion-dollar corporation. In 1902 Morgan brought together several of the leading agricultural-equipment manufacturers to form the International Harvester Company. In that same year he organized, with less subsequent success, the International Merchant Marine, an amalgamation of a majority of the transatlantic shipping lines.

Morgan successfully led the American financial community's attempt to avert a general financial collapse following the stock market panic of 1907. He headed a group of bankers who took in large government deposits and decided how the money was to be used for purposes of financial relief, thereby preserving the solvency of many major banks and corporations. Having ceased to undertake large industrial reorganizations, Morgan thereafter concentrated on amassing control of various banks and insurance companies. Through a system of interlocking memberships on the boards of companies he had reorganized or influenced, Morgan and his banking house achieved a top-heavy concentration of control over some of the nation's leading corporations and financial institutions. This earned Morgan the occasional distrust of the federal government and the enmity of reformers and muckrakers throughout the country, but he remained the dominant figure in American capitalism until his death in Rome on March 31, 1913.

Morgan was one of the greatest art and book collectors of his day, and he donated many works of art to the

Metropolitan Museum of Art in New York City. His book collection and the building that housed them in New York City became a public reference library in 1924.

JAMES J. HILL

James J. Hill was a financier and railroad builder of the American Northwest.

James Jerome Hill was born on Sept. 16, 1838, near Guelph, Ont., Can. After settling in St. Paul, Minn., about 1870, he established transportation lines on the Mississippi and Red rivers and arranged a traffic interchange with the St. Paul and Pacific Railroad. On that line's failure in 1873, Hill interested Canadian capitalists and reorganized it as the St. Paul, Minneapolis, and Manitoba Railway Company, becoming its president in 1882.

After the Great Northern Railway absorbed the St. Paul line in 1890, Hill became its president (1893–1907) and chairman of its board of directors (1907–12). The Northern Pacific and the Chicago, Burlington and Quincy railroads also came under Hill's control.

He was active in banking as president of the Northern Securities Company (which in 1904 was declared in violation of the Sherman Anti-Trust Act). In 1912 he took control of the First and Second National Banks of St. Paul and effected a merger. His *Highways of Progress* was published in 1910. Hill died on May 29, 1916, in St. Paul.

THE CENTRAL PACIFIC AND SOUTHERN PACIFIC RAILROADS

The Central Pacific Railroad and Southern Pacific were two great Western railroads founded in the 1860s by a group of California merchants known later as the "Big Four" of Western railroad building—Collis P. Huntington,

Leland Stanford, Mark Hopkins, and Charles Crocker. They are best remembered for the Central Pacific, which built part of the first American transcontinental rail line.

The Central Pacific line was first conceived in 1861 and surveyed by an engineer, Theodore Dehone Judah, who obtained the financial backing of the California group and won federal support in the form of the Pacific Railway Act (1862), which provided land grants and subsidies to both the Central Pacific and the Union Pacific. Each company was granted financial support from government bonds and awarded sizable parcels of land along the entire length of their route as an added incentive.

Huntington represented the Central Pacific in the East, handling the financing and purchasing and acting as political lobbyist. Crocker was in charge of construction. Stanford, who was governor of California in 1861–63, saw to the company's financial and political interests in the West. The associates subscribed some of their own funds initially, but most of the capital for the actual construction came from public funds and grants. All four men became enormously wealthy. (Stanford went on to found Stanford University.)

The Central Pacific began laying track eastward from Sacramento, Calif., in 1863, and the Union Pacific started westward from Omaha, Neb., two years later. To meet its manpower needs, the Central Pacific hired thousands of Chinese labourers, including many recruited from farms in Canton. The crew had the formidable task of laying the track that crossed the rugged Sierra Nevada mountain range, blasting nine tunnels to accomplish this. Meanwhile the crew of the Union Pacific, composed largely of Irish immigrants and Civil War veterans, had to contend with Indian attacks and the Rocky Mountains. On May 10, 1869, after completing 1,800 miles (2,900 km) of new track, the two rail lines met at Promontory, Utah.

Having completed the transcontinental line, the Big Four started the Southern Pacific as a branch line of the Central Pacific into southern California. It reached the Arizona border in 1877, and in 1883 it was joined to other railroads built west from New Orleans, Louisiana, across Texas and New Mexico. These lines were collectively known as the Central Pacific system. On March 17, 1884, a new Southern Pacific Company was incorporated (under a special Kentucky charter) to act as a holding company for the several operating railroads, and the railroads making up the Central Pacific system were leased to it a year later. The Central Pacific thus became the nucleus from which the Southern Pacific system developed; the two companies merged in 1959. The Southern Pacific served 15 states in the West and Southwest, including the Pacific and Gulf coasts, with the network dipping south from northwestern Oregon to swing in a wide arc up into Illinois. The railroad served 35 international points of entry. About half the railroad's freight revenues came from food products, lumber, chemicals, and motor vehicles.

In 1971, along with many other railroads, the Southern Pacific gave up operating intercity passenger trains, although it continued to operate several long-distance trains for the federally sponsored National Railroad Passenger Corporation (Amtrak). In 1983 the Southern Pacific Transportation Company, a holding company for the railroad, agreed to merge with the holding company of the Atchison, Topeka and Santa Fe Railway, but in 1987 the Interstate Commerce Commission rejected the proposed merger, and in 1988 the Southern Pacific was sold to Rio Grande Industries, owner and operator of the Denver and Rio Grande Western Railroad system. The Southern Pacific was acquired by the Union Pacific Corporation in 1996. The merged firm represents the largest railroad company in the United States and controls most of the rail-based shipping in the western two-thirds of the country.

COLLIS P. HUNTINGTON

Collis Potter Huntington was one of the Big Four railroad magnates in California who promoted the Central Pacific Railroad's extension across the West, making possible the first transcontinental railroad in 1869.

Born into a poor family on Oct. 22, 1821, in Harwinton, Conn., Huntington worked as an itinerant peddler and became a prosperous merchant in Oneonta, N.Y., before moving to Sacramento, Calif., in the gold rush year of 1849. There he became a partner with Mark Hopkins in a successful wholesale-retail firm that specialized in miners' supplies. In the late 1850s he became interested in a plan to link California with the eastern United States by rail, and he joined Hopkins, Leland Stanford, and Charles Crocker in their joint incorporation of the Central Pacific Railroad in 1861, which was soon designated as the western part of the projected transcontinental railroad.

During the actual construction (1863–69) of the Central Pacific Railroad, Huntington lobbied for the company in the East, working to secure financing and favourable legislation from Congress and the federal government. In 1865 the Big Four formed the Southern Pacific Railroad, which constructed rail lines down southern California and across the Southwest to New Orleans, again with Huntington serving as chief political and financial lobbyist. Huntington helped expand the Southern Pacific Railroad into a 9,600-mile (15,450-km) line that was the foundation of rail service in California and the western link for a southern transcontinental rail route. He also extended the lines of the Chesapeake and Ohio Railway, which he had bought in 1869, to link with the

Southern Pacific, forming a 4,000-mile (6,400-km) continuous track from San Francisco to Newport News, Va.

Huntington became president of the Southern Pacific–Central Pacific rail system in 1890 and thus controlled a vast empire of rail lines and agricultural landholdings in California until his death on Aug. 13, 1900, at Raquette Lake, N.Y.

LELAND STANFORD

Amasa Leland Stanford was a political leader in California and one of the builders of the first U.S. transcontinental railroad.

Stanford was born on March 9, 1824, in Watervliet, N.Y. He practiced law in Port Washington, Wis., from 1848 to 1852, before moving to Sacramento, Calif., where he achieved much success in retailing mining supplies and general merchandise. He also became active in local politics. A Republican, he served as governor of California from 1861 to 1863.

Stanford invested heavily in the plan to build a transcontinental railroad, and, when the Central Pacific Railroad was organized in 1861, he became its president (1861–93). He was instrumental in the success of the Central Pacific, which was built eastward to join with the Union Pacific at Promontory, Utah, in 1869. He also played a major role in railroad development throughout California and the Southwest. From 1885 until his death on June 21, 1893, in Palo Alto, he served in the U.S. Senate. Stanford and his wife, Jane, founded Stanford University in 1885.

MARK HOPKINS

Mark Hopkins was a capitalist who helped build the Central Pacific (and later the Southern Pacific) Railroad.

Hopkins was born on Sept. 3, 1814, in Richmond County, Va. After his birth, his family settled in North Carolina. In 1845 he and his brother Moses left home for Kentucky and, when news of the gold rush reached them, moved on to California (May 1851). By the spring of 1852 Hopkins had given up unprofitable gold mining and started a grocery business in Placerville and, the next year, in Sacramento. In 1855 he joined with another Sacramento merchant, Collis P. Huntington, to form Huntington & Hopkins, which became one of the most prosperous mercantile houses in the state. In 1861 the two men were approached by an enterprising engineer, Theodore Dehone Judah, who envisaged a new transcontinental railroad; and in June a company called the Central Pacific Railroad was organized, with Hopkins, Huntington, and fellow merchants Leland Stanford and Charles Crocker as the major directors (the "Big Four"). In 1869 the main line was completed, meeting the Union Pacific at Promontory, Utah; feeder lines were soon added throughout California.

Hopkins' three partners eventually moved to San Francisco, and he began building a spectacular mansion there atop Nob Hill (at the site of the present-day Mark Hopkins Hotel). He remained in Sacramento, however, and the house was not completed until after his death on March 29, 1878, in Yuma, Arizona Territory, about a week after arriving to seek a health cure in the desert.

CHARLES CROCKER

Businessman and banker Charles Crocker was a chief contractor in the building of the Central Pacific (and later the Southern Pacific) Railroad.

Born on Sept. 16, 1822, in Troy, N.Y., Crocker was forced to quit school at an early age to help support his family. After his family moved to Indiana, he did various jobs—farming, working in a sawmill, and serving as an apprentice in a blacksmith shop and foundry. Finally, he and his brothers Clark and Henry migrated overland to California (1850) after gold was discovered there. Crocker abandoned his attempt at prospecting in 1852 and opened a store in Sacramento, becoming extremely wealthy by 1854. In 1855 he was elected to the city council and, in 1860, to the state legislature, as a Republican.

In 1861 Crocker joined fellow merchants Collis P. Huntington, Leland Stanford, and Mark Hopkins (known collectively as the "Big Four") in a new railway company, the Central Pacific, which was appointed to build the western portion of the first American transcontinental railroad. Crocker became the contractor in charge of construction, hiring men and equipment, setting up campsites, and acting as paymaster and accountant. He was responsible for importing Chinese labourers (the "coolie system"). The line that he started building on Feb. 22, 1863, met the Union Pacific line, running from the east, at Promontory Point, Utah, on May 10, 1869.

In 1871 he became president of the Southern Pacific Railroad of California and, in 1884, oversaw the new incorporation of Southern Pacific, which absorbed the Central Pacific. Crocker also engaged in real estate, industrial properties, and banking (his Crocker First National Bank of San Francisco, chartered in 1870, was an ancestor of the modern Crocker National Bank, which merged with Wells Fargo & Company in 1986). He built a showplace mansion in San Francisco (which burned down in 1906) and a second home in New York City. He died on Aug. 14, 1888, in Monterey, Calif. His fortune at his death was estimated at $40 million.

THE UNION PACIFIC RAILROAD

The Union Pacific Railroad Company, incorporated by an act of the U.S. Congress on July 1, 1862, was one of the companies that extended the American railway system to the Pacific coast. The original Union Pacific rail line was built westward 1,006 miles (1,619 km) from Omaha, Neb., to meet the Central Pacific, which was being built eastward from Sacramento, Calif. The two railroads were joined at Promontory, Utah, on May 10, 1869.

The Union Pacific was largely financed by federal loans and land grants, but it overextended itself through its involvement in the Crédit Mobilier scandal. Crédit Mobilier was part of a complex arrangement whereby a few men contracted with themselves or assignees for the construction of the railroad. Experience had already taught veteran railroad organizers that more money could be made from construction contracts than from operating the completed road. This promised to be doubly true in the case of the Union Pacific, which was supported by federal loans and land grants but would be spanning the vast unpopulated region between Omaha, on the Missouri River, and Great Salt Lake—a territory unlikely to produce much immediate revenue. Along with certain trustees, the manipulators reaped enormous profits but impoverished the railroad in the process. When it was revealed that Oakes Ames, a congressman from Massachusetts, was involved, the House of Representatives investigated the scandal and censured him and a colleague; several others, including Vice Pres. Schuyler Colfax, were absolved.

After exposure of the scheme, which left the railroad badly in debt, the company went into receivership in 1893. It was reorganized in 1897 under the leadership of Edward H. Harriman, who was responsible for major improvements and standardization and who led the railroad to participate in the economic development of the West. Harriman used the railroad as a holding company for the securities of other transportation companies in his empire. His son, W. Averell Harriman, was chairman of the board of Union Pacific from 1932 to 1946.

The Union Pacific grew to operate in 13 western states, extending from Council Bluffs, Iowa, and Kansas City, Mo., to Portland, Ore., and Los Angeles. Since 1969 it has been owned by the Union Pacific Corporation, a holding company.

In 1982 the Union Pacific merged with two other railroads, the Missouri Pacific Railroad Company (headquartered in St. Louis, Missouri) and the Western Pacific Railroad Company (headquartered in San Francisco), to form what came to be called the Union Pacific System. Western Pacific became a subsidiary of Union Pacific at this time, while Union Pacific and Missouri Pacific retained their separate corporate identities until the merger was completed in 1997. At that time, traffic control and marketing for all three railroads were fully unified, and all lines operated under the Union Pacific name. With its acquisition of the Southern Pacific Rail Corporation in 1996, the Union Pacific became the largest domestic railroad in the United States, controlling almost all of the rail-based shipping in the western two-thirds of the country. It carries products and commodities such as coal, automobiles, foods, forest and agricultural products, and chemicals and is one of the largest intermodal shippers (including truck trailers and containers) in the country. Corporate headquarters are in Omaha, where the Union Pacific laid its first rails in 1865.

OAKES AMES

Oakes Ames, a successful businessman and politician, was a leading figure in the Crédit Mobilier scandal following the American Civil War.

Ames was born on Jan. 10, 1804, in Easton, Mass. He left school at age 16 to enter his father's shovel company, Oliver Ames & Sons. Assuming progressively more responsible positions in the firm, he eventually took over management of the company (along with his brother Oliver [1807–77]) upon his father's retirement in 1844.

The gold rushes in California and Australia, along with agricultural development of the Mississippi Valley, created enormous demand for Ames's shovels. By the outbreak of the Civil War, the business was worth $4 million. Drawn to the Republican Party by his ardent beliefs in free soil and free enterprise, Ames ran for a Massachusetts congressional seat in 1862. He won—and then won reelection four times. He was, however, an inconspicuous member of the House.

In 1865, along with brother Oliver and railroad executive T.C. Durant, Ames helped create the Crédit Mobilier of America—a company formed to build the Union Pacific Railroad. The Crédit Mobilier allowed a small number of individuals to reap vast fortunes from the construction of the line. By early 1868, Congress seemed certain to investigate charges of improper use of government grants to the railroad. But Ames, through shrewd sale of Crédit Mobilier stock at bargain prices to appropriate members of Congress, induced his colleagues to abandon the investigation.

A quarrel between Ames and a Crédit Mobilier investor led, in 1872, to the publication of documents detailing Ames's misuse of company stock to derail the congressional investigation of 1868. An immediate congressional investigation ensued, concluding with a vote of 182–36 in favour of censuring Ames. He returned to Easton and died a disgraced and broken figure on May 8, 1873.

EDWARD H. HARRIMAN

Edward Henry Harriman, a financier and railroad magnate, was one of the leading builders and organizers in the era of great railroad expansion and development of the West during the late 19th century.

Harriman was born on Feb. 25, 1848, in Hempstead, N.Y. He became a broker's clerk in New York at an early age and in 1870 was able to buy a seat on the New York Stock Exchange on his own account. His career in railroad management started with executive positions with the Illinois Central. In 1898 his career as a great railway organizer began with his formation, by the aid of the bankers Kuhn, Loeb & Co., of a syndicate to acquire the Union Pacific Railroad Company, which was then in receivership. Having brought the Union Pacific out of bankruptcy into prosperity, he utilized his position to draw other lines within his control, notably the Southern Pacific in 1901. His abortive contest in 1901 with James J. Hill for the control of the Northern Pacific led to one of the most serious financial crises ever known on Wall Street. At his death on Sept. 9, 1909, near Turner, N.Y., Harriman's influence was estimated to extend over 60,000 miles (100,000 km) of track. His business methods excited bitter criticism, culminating in a stern denunciation from Pres. Theodore Roosevelt in 1907.

The history of bridge design is full of great names, and some of the greatest of them worked on structures that enabled railroads to cross open chasms or bodies of water. Some of those individuals are profiled below.

THE 19TH CENTURY

The 19th century was a period of heroic bridge work, a time when structures were erected that had never before been dreamed of or thought possible. The design of these structures and the organizing of the effort to build them can often be credited to single individuals of exceptional vision and ability.

ROBERT STEPHENSON

Robert Stephenson was an outstanding English Victorian civil engineer and builder of many long-span railroad bridges, most notably the Britannia Bridge over the Menai Strait, North Wales.

The only son of George Stephenson, inventor of the railroad locomotive, Robert was born on Oct. 16, 1803, in Willington Quay, Northumberland. He was educated at Bruce's Academy, Newcastle upon Tyne, and at Edinburgh University. In 1821 he assisted his father in survey work for the Stockton and Darlington Railway and afterward on the Liverpool and Manchester Railway. After serving as a mining engineer in Colombia, he returned to

England, where he made many improvements in loco-motives and in 1833 was appointed chief engineer of the London and Birmingham Railway. In this position he directed several major engineering works, such as the cut-ting, or excavation, at Blisworth and the Kilsby Tunnel. Next undertaking a new railroad line from Newcastle to Berwick, he spanned the Tyne River with a six-arch iron bridge, using James Nasmyth's newly invented steam ham-mer to drive the bridge's foundations.

Called on to build a secure railroad bridge over the Menai Strait, between the Isle of Anglesey and the Welsh mainland, Stephenson conceived a unique tubular design, the success of which led to several other tubular bridges built by Stephenson in England and other countries. Stephenson died on Oct. 12, 1859, in London.

WILLIAM FAIRBAIRN

William Fairbairn was a Scottish civil engineer and inven-tor who did pioneering work in bridge design and in testing iron and finding new applications for it.

Fairbairn was born on Feb. 19, 1789, in Kelso, Roxburghshire [now in Scottish Borders], Scot. From 1817 to 1832 he was a millwright at Manchester, in partnership with James Lillie. In 1835 he established a shipbuilding yard at Millwall, London, where he constructed several hundred vessels. In 1844 he introduced the Lancashire boiler with twin flues. He was the first to use wrought iron for ship hulls, bridges, mill shafting, and structural beams. He also experimented with the strength of iron and the relative merits of hot and cold blast in iron manufacture. In 1845 he joined Robert Stephenson in designing two tubular railway bridges in Wales: the Britannia Bridge, spanning the Menai Strait, and the Conwy Bridge over the River Conwy. The Britannia Bridge, employing a type of box girder or plate girder that came into worldwide use, was partly riveted by hydraulic machines designed by Fairbairn.

Fairbairn became Sir William Fairbairn, 1st Baronet, in 1869. His youngest brother, Sir Peter (1799–1861), founded in Leeds an establishment to make textile machinery and machine tools and was knighted in 1858. Sir William died on Aug. 18, 1874, in Moor Park, Surrey, Eng.

ISAMBARD KINGDOM BRUNEL

Isambard Kingdom Brunel was a British civil and mechanical engineer of great originality who built bridges, railways, and tunnels and designed the first transatlantic steamer.

Brunel was born on April 9, 1806, in Portsmouth, Hampshire, Eng. The only son of the engineer and inventor Sir Marc Isambard Brunel, he was appointed resident engineer when work on the Thames Tunnel began, under his father's direction, in 1825. He held the post until 1828, when a sudden inundation seriously injured him and brought the tunnel work to a standstill that financial problems stretched to seven years. While recuperating, he prepared designs for a suspension bridge over the Avon Gorge in Bristol, one of which was ultimately adopted in the construction of the Clifton Suspension Bridge (1830–63) in preference to a design by the noted Scottish engineer Thomas Telford.

As engineer at the Bristol Docks, Brunel carried out extensive improvements. He designed the Monkwearmouth Docks in 1831 and, later, similar works at Brentford, Briton Ferry, Milford Haven, and Plymouth. In 1833 he was appointed chief engineer to the Great Western Railway. His introduction of the broad-gauge railway (rails 7 feet [2 metres] apart) provoked the famous "battle of the gauges." The broad gauge made possible high speeds that were a great stimulus to railway progress. In 1844 he introduced a system of pneumatic propulsion on the South Devon Railway, but the experiment was a failure.

Brunel was responsible for building more than 1,000 miles (1,600 km) of railway in the West Country, the Midlands, South Wales, and Ireland. He constructed two railway lines in Italy and was an adviser on the construction of the Victorian lines in Australia and the Eastern Bengal Railway in India. His first notable railway works were the Box Tunnel and the Maidenhead Bridge, and his last were the Chepstow and Saltash (Royal Albert) bridges, all in England. The Maidenhead Bridge had the flattest brick arch in the world. His use of a compressed-air caisson to sink the pier foundations for the bridge helped gain acceptance of compressed-air techniques in underwater and underground construction.

Brunel made outstanding contributions to marine engineering with his three ships, the *Great Western* (1837), *Great Britain* (1843), and *Great Eastern* (originally called *Leviathan;* 1858), each the largest in the world at its date of launching. The *Great Western,* a wooden paddle vessel, was the first steamship to provide regular transatlantic service. The *Great Britain,* an iron-hull steamship, was the first large vessel driven by a screw propeller. The *Great Eastern* was propelled by both paddles and screw and was the first ship to utilize a double iron hull. Unsurpassed in size for 40 years, the *Great Eastern* was not a success as a passenger ship but achieved fame by laying the first successful transatlantic cable.

Brunel worked on the improvement of large guns and designed a floating armoured barge used for the attack on Kronshtadt in 1854 during the Crimean War. He also designed a complete prefabricated hospital building that was shipped in parts to the Crimea in 1855. He died on Sept. 15, 1859, in Westminster, London.

CHARLES ELLET

Charles Ellet was an engineer who built the first wire-cable suspension bridge in America.

Ellet was born on Jan. 1, 1810, in Penn's Manor, Pa. After working for three years as a surveyor and assistant engineer, he studied at the École des Ponts et Chaussées, Paris, and traveled in France, Switzerland, and Great Britain, studying engineering works. After he returned to the United States in 1832, he proposed to Congress a 1,000-foot (300-metre) suspension bridge over the Potomac River at Washington, D.C. Like several of his early projects, this plan was too advanced for its time and was generally discouraged. In 1842 Ellet completed his wire-cable suspension bridge over the Schuylkill River at Philadelphia. Supported by five wire cables on each side, the bridge had a span of 358 feet (109 metres).

Ellet designed and built (1846–49) for the Baltimore & Ohio Railway the world's first long-span wire-cable suspension bridge over the Ohio River at Wheeling, Va. The central span of 1,010 feet (308 metres) was then the longest ever built.

In 1847 Ellet contracted to build a bridge over the Niagara River, 2 miles (3 km) below the falls. A light suspension span was built as a service bridge, and over it Ellet became the first man to ride across the Niagara Gorge. A dispute over money led Ellet to resign in 1848, leaving the bridge uncompleted.

After the outbreak of the American Civil War, Ellet devised a steam-powered ram that played a role in winning domination of the Mississippi River by the Union. He personally led a fleet of nine rams in the Battle of Memphis on June 6, 1862. Union forces were victorious, but Ellet was mortally wounded. He died on June 21, 1862, at Cairo, Ill.

JAMES EADS

James Buchanan Eads was an American engineer best known for his triple-arch steel bridge over the Mississippi River at St. Louis, Mo. (1874).

Eads was born on May 23, 1820, in Lawrenceburg, Ind. He was named for his mother's cousin James Buchanan, a Pennsylvania congressman who later became president of the United States. The boy spent a migrant youth with little formal education, for his father's never very successful business ventures took the family to Cincinnati, Ohio, then Louisville, Ky., and finally St. Louis. James Eads educated himself by reading the library of his first employer, a St. Louis dry-goods merchant. At 18 he became purser on a Mississippi riverboat. Not long after, he began to consider means to recover by salvage the heavy losses from the frequent riverboat disasters. When he was 22, he invented a salvage boat, which he called a submarine; actually it was a surface vessel from which he could descend in a diving bell he had also designed and walk the river bottom. He recovered lead and iron pigs and other valuable freight; on one occasion he retrieved a cargo that included a large crock of butter in a good state of preservation. So successful was his equipment that in 12 years of operations on the Mississippi and its tributaries he made his fortune.

Retiring from the river to marry and settle down, Eads set himself up briefly as a glass manufacturer, but the promising enterprise, the first glass factory in the West, was ruined by the Mexican War; by 1848 he was back in the salvage business. He built three new submarines, the third of which was capable of pumping out and raising a sunken hull from the bottom. Within a few years he had 10 boats in his fleet.

As the Civil War threatened, Eads foresaw the struggle that would take place for control of the Mississippi system, and he advanced a radical idea. He proposed that ironclad steam-powered warships of shallow draft be built to operate on the rivers. The U.S. government was slow to take up his offer to build such a flotilla; when it did, he built the ships in record time, working 4,000 men on day and night shifts seven days a week. The novel craft he set afloat spearheaded Grant's offensive against Forts Henry and Donelson, the first important Union victories of the war. They continued to play a conspicuous role under Andrew Foote and David Farragut at Memphis, Island No. 10, Vicksburg, and Mobile Bay. The vessels were the first ironclads to fight in North America and the first in the world to engage enemy warships. (The *Monitor* and *Merrimack,* both ironclads that battled in the American Civil War, were the first such vessels to close against each other in combat.)

Immediately after the war, Eads was chosen to direct a construction project of extraordinary difficulty, the bridging of the Mississippi at St. Louis. From his knowledge of the river and of the fabrication of iron and steel, he secured, against opposition, some of it unscrupulous, a contract for a steel triple-arch bridge over the river at St. Louis, which he began on Aug. 20, 1867. Its three spans, 502, 520, and 502 feet (152, 158, and 152 metres), respectively, consisted of triangularly braced 18-inch (46-cm) hollow steel tubes linked in units and set in piers based on bedrock. Since the rock lay some 100 feet (30 metres) below the river surface, reaching it posed major problems. The work of digging through the mud bottom had to be carried on under compressed air, and some of the men developed decompression sickness (the bends). After two workers died on March 19, 1870, Eads established a floating hospital, provided nourishing food for his workers, insisted on slow decompression on emerging from the caissons, and installed a lift.

The steel used in construction of the bridge was subject to similar rigorous standards; it was inspected at the works and on the site. Indeed, its supplier, the famed industrialist Andrew Carnegie, was forced to take back some batches for rerolling three times, and some were still rejected as not conforming to the specified strength of 60,000 pounds (27,000 kg) per square inch. Many other problems arose. To construct his first steel arches without disturbing navigation on the river, Eads used timber cantilevers to support them, with the halves of each arch held back by cables passing over the top of towers built on the piers. To join the two halves of the middle arch, Eads's deputy, Colonel Henry Flad, had planned to hump the middle arch slightly to bring the two halves together; then, with the cantilevering removed, the arch would assume its normal shape. Eads, on the other hand, had prepared a wrought-iron plug fitted with threads; the last two arch ribs could be shortened by 5 inches (13 cm) each and cut with screw threads to receive the plug, which would close the distance between the ribs. Because of an unusual mid-September warm spell, which warped the bridge arches toward the north, Flad could not close the arches by the method he had chosen and, after trying to cool the steel tubes with ice packs, fell back on Eads's screw-plug connection. The first arch was closed on Sept. 17, 1873.

The Eads, or St. Louis, Bridge, the largest bridge of any type built up to that time, was recognized throughout the world as a landmark engineering achievement, with its pioneering use of structural steel, its foundations planted at record depths, and its cantilevering technique used for raising the arches. The bridge was officially opened on July 4, 1874.

Soon after, Eads's rare understanding of the Mississippi was enlisted at New Orleans to provide a year-round navigation channel for the city. Despite widespread skepticism, he successfully altered the sedimental behaviour of the river by building a series of jetties, and within five years, by 1879, he had created a practical channel for shipping. In this important work he employed a technique of carrying out the project at his own expense, simply on the basis of guarantees if successful. On the same conditions he sought to promote a ship-carrying railway across the Isthmus of Tehuantepec, in Mexico, as a more economic and viable alternative to a canal across the Isthmus of Panama. Two bills to promote the railway, however, failed in Congress.

James Buchanan Eads was the first U.S. engineer to be honoured with the Albert Medal of the Royal Society of Arts in London. He had been a consultant for Liverpool docks, as well as for installations in Toronto and in Veracruz and Tampico, Mex. Twice married, he had two daughters and three stepdaughters. He died on March 8, 1887, in Nassau, Bahamas.

BENJAMIN BAKER

English civil engineer Benjamin Baker was the chief designer of the railway bridge over the Firth of Forth, Scotland.

Baker was born on March 31, 1840, in Keyford, Somerset, Eng. In 1861 he became an assistant to the consulting engineer John Fowler and by 1875 was his partner. Baker became Fowler's chief assistant in 1869 and as such was responsible for the construction of the subterranean District Railway from Westminster to the City of London. He also served as consultant for the building of other London Underground lines, all bored deep in the London clay. His other projects included the docks at Avonmouth and Hull and the ocean transport (1878) of the 180-ton obelisk Cleopatra's Needle from Egypt and its reerection in London.

In 1867 Baker wrote a series of articles, "Long Span Bridges," discussing the application of cantilevers, which were later used in his Forth Bridge (1882–90). At the completion of that bridge, Baker was knighted. He served on numerous government commissions and boards and, among other assignments as a consultant, implemented William Willcocks's plans for the Aswān Dam (1898–1902). In the United States he was consulted by James B. Eads on the construction of his steel bridge over the Mississippi River at St. Louis, Mo., and, when the first Hudson River tunnel threatened to fail, Baker was called in to design a tunneling shield that allowed work to be completed. Baker was president of the Institution of Civil Engineers in 1895–96 and a vice president of the Royal Society from 1896 to his death on May 19, 1907, in Pangbourne, Berkshire.

JOHN FOWLER

English civil engineer John Fowler helped design and build the underground London Metropolitan Railway and was joint designer, with Benjamin Baker, of the Forth Bridge in Scotland.

Fowler was born on July 15, 1817, in Wadsley, near Sheffield, Yorkshire, Eng. He established himself in London in 1844 as a consulting engineer, laying out many small railway systems later incorporated into the Manchester, Sheffield, and Lincolnshire railways. In 1860 he completed the Pimlico Bridge across the Thames River, one of the first railway bridges in the area. He worked on most of the extensions of the Metropolitan Railway (the early London Underground), which was the world's first subway system. Its lines were excavated from the surface and permanently covered rather than tunneled. He also designed and built a locomotive known as "Fowler's Ghost" for the railway. Later he was an engineer for the deep-tunneling "tube" system extensively adopted for London electric railways. He was also the engineer for the construction of Victoria Station, and in 1866–67 he was president of the Institution of Civil Engineers.

After serving as general engineering adviser in Egypt to the khedive Ismā'īl, he became in 1875 a partner of Benjamin Baker, with whom he designed and constructed the great cantilever bridge over the Firth of Forth (1882–90). He was created a baronet in 1890. Sir John Fowler died on Nov. 20, 1898, on Bournemouth, Hampshire.

JOHN AUGUSTUS ROEBLING

John Augustus Roebling was a German-born American civil engineer, a pioneer in the design of steel suspension bridges. His best-known work is the Brooklyn Bridge, New York City, completed under the direction of his eldest son, Washington Augustus, in 1883.

John Augustus Roebling.
Photos.com/Jupiterimages

Roebling was born on June 12, 1806, in Mühlhausen, Prussia. After graduating from the polytechnic school in Berlin, Roebling worked for the Prussian government for three years and at the age of 25 immigrated to the United States. He settled with others from his hometown in a small colony that was later called Saxonburg, near

Pittsburgh, in the hills of western Pennsylvania. He married the daughter of another Mühlhausen immigrant, and they had nine children. After a few years of unsuccessful farming, John Roebling went to the state capital in Harrisburg and applied for employment as a civil engineer.

He had often watched canalboats being hauled over hills from one watershed to another, and he persuaded the canal commissioners to let him replace the hempen hawsers with wire cables. He developed his own method for stranding and weaving wire cables, which proved to be as strong and durable as he had predicted. The demand for such cable soon became so great that he established a factory to manufacture it in Trenton, N.J. This was the beginning of an industrial complex that finally was capable of producing everything from chicken wire to enormous 36-inch (91-cm) cables. It remained a family-owned business, carried on by three generations of Roeblings.

Roebling was less a businessman than an engineer, and with the growth of his reputation as a designer and builder of long-span suspension bridges, he spent less and less time at the Trenton factory. His eldest son, Washington, joined him in his work, and in the 1850s and 1860s they built four suspension bridges: two at Pittsburgh, one at Niagara Falls, and another across the Ohio River between Cincinnati, Ohio, and Covington, Ky., with a main span of 1,051 feet (320 metres). New York state accepted Roebling's design for a bridge connecting Brooklyn and Manhattan with a span of 1,595 ft (486 metres) and appointed him chief engineer.

Work on the bridge cost Roebling his life. He was taking final compass readings while standing on some pilings at a ferry slip and did not notice that a boat was docking. As it banged into the slip, one of his feet was caught between the pilings. He was rushed to his son's house in Brooklyn Heights, where the doctors amputated his injured toes. Three weeks later, on July 22, 1869, he died of tetanus at the age of 63. His son carried on his work on the Brooklyn Bridge.

GUSTAVE EIFFEL

Alexandre-Gustave Eiffel was a French civil engineer renowned for the tower in Paris that bears his name.

Eiffel was born on Dec. 15, 1832, in Dijon, France. After graduation from the College of Art and Manufacturing in 1855, he began to specialize in metal construction, especially bridges. He directed the erection of an iron bridge at Bordeaux in 1858, followed by several others, and designed the lofty, arched Gallery of Machines for the Paris Exhibition of 1867. In 1877 he bridged the Douro River at Oporto, Port., with a 525-foot (160-metre) steel arch, which he followed with an even greater arch of the same type, the 540-foot (162-metre) span Garabit viaduct over the Truyère River in southern France, for many years the highest bridge in the world, 400 feet (120 metres) over the stream. He was one of the first engineers to employ compressed-air caissons in bridge building. He designed the movable dome of the observatory at Nice and the framework of the Statue of Liberty in New York Harbor.

Eiffel startled the world with the construction of the Eiffel Tower (1887–89), which brought him the nickname "magician of iron." It also directed his interest to problems of aerodynamics, and he used the tower for a number of experiments. At Auteuil, outside Paris, he built the first aerodynamic laboratory, where he continued to work throughout World War I; in 1921 he gave the laboratory to the state. Eiffel died on Dec. 28, 1923, in Paris.

THE 20TH CENTURY

In the 20th century, bridge designers built upon the great achievements of the previous century and constructed bridges of greater length and technical sophistication, frequently making use of new materials and analytical tools that had not been available to their predecessors.

GUSTAV LINDENTHAL

Austrian-born American civil engineer Gustav Lindenthal is known for designing Hell Gate Bridge across New York City's East River.

Lindenthal was born on May 21, 1850, in Brünn, Austria (now Brno, Czech Rep.). After gaining experience working on railways and bridges in Austria and Switzerland, he immigrated to the United States (1871). He served as a construction engineer at the Philadelphia Centennial Exposition (1874–77) and then went to Pittsburgh as a consulting engineer in railway and bridge construction.

In 1890 he moved to New York City, where he became commissioner of bridges (1902–03). There he designed and acted as consulting engineer for the Hell Gate Railway bridge, which opened for traffic in March 1917. At that time Hell Gate was the longest (977 feet [298 metres]) steel arch in the world. Lindenthal designed the Queensboro (cantilever) Bridge, also over the East River, and was a consulting engineer for railroad tunnels under the Hudson and East rivers. He died on July 31, 1935, in Metuchen, N.J.

OTHMAR AMMANN

Othmar Herman Amman was a Swiss-born American engineer and designer of numerous long suspension bridges, including the Verrazano-Narrows Bridge over New York harbour, at its completion (1965) the longest single span in the world.

Amman was born on March 26, 1879, in Schaffhausen, Switz. In 1904 Ammann immigrated to the United States, where he helped design railroad bridges. Joining the Pennsylvania Steel Company the following year, he worked on the Queensboro Bridge, New York City. During his term (1912–23) as chief assistant to the noted bridge engineer Gustav Lindenthal, he helped design and build the Hell Gate (steel arch) Bridge, New York City, and the Ohio River Bridge, Sciotoville, Ohio.

In 1923 Ammann set up his own engineering firm in New York City, and the following year the Port of New York Authority agreed to finance his proposed bridge across the Hudson River between New Jersey and upper Manhattan. When finished in 1931, the George Washington Bridge was the longest in the world, almost double the length of the previous record holder.

Ammann was chief engineer of the Port of New York Authority from 1930 to 1937 and director of engineering from 1937 to 1939. As chief engineer, he was in charge of building the Bayonne Bridge over the Kill van Kull, N.J., the Outerbridge Crossing and Goethals Bridge across Arthur Kill, and the Lincoln Tunnel under the Hudson River. As director of engineering, he directed the building of the Bronx-Whitestone Bridge and the Triborough Bridge (later renamed the Robert F. Kennedy Bridge), New York City. He also sat on the Board of Engineers in charge of San Francisco's Golden Gate Bridge, which opened in 1937.

In 1939 Ammann returned to private practice, designing bridges and highways in New Jersey and New York. He served on the three-man board that investigated the Tacoma Narrows Bridge aerodynamic failure in 1941. In partnership with Charles S. Whitney from 1946, Ammann designed the Throgs Neck Bridge, New York City, the Dulles International Airport, outside Washington, D.C., and three buildings for New York City's Lincoln Center for the Performing Arts. He died on Sept. 22, 1965, in Rye, N.Y.

RALPH FREEMAN

Ralph Freeman was an English civil engineer whose Sydney Harbour Bridge (1932), New South Wales, with a main arch span of 1,650 feet (500 metres), is one of the longest steel-arch bridges in the world.

Freeman was born on Nov. 27, 1880, in London. In 1901 he joined a London firm of consulting engineers, later known as Freeman, Fox & Partners. His works include the Victoria Falls Bridge over the Zambezi River, on the border of present-day Zimbabwe and Zambia; the Royal Naval Propellant factory built during World War II; the Furness shipbuilding yard in Lancashire; and five major bridges in southern Africa. He also prepared designs for the bridge over Auckland Harbour, New Zealand.

From 1928 to 1936 he was a member of the Steel Structures Research Committee, a British organization, and chairman of the panel responsible for effecting the committee's designs. He was knighted in 1947. Sir Ralph Freeman died on March 11, 1950, in London.

RALPH MODJESKI

Ralph Modjeski was a Polish-born American bridge designer and builder, outstanding for the number, variety, and innovative character of his projects.

Modjeski was born on Jan. 27, 1861, in Kraków, Pol. He was the son of the actress Helena Modjeska (1840–1909).

The Huey P. Long Bridge spanning the Mississippi River in Jefferson Parish, La.; Ralph Modjeski was chief engineer of the bridge. Shawn Graham/U.S. Navy Photo

After study in Paris, he settled in the United States and from 1892 practiced as a consulting bridge engineer in Chicago.

Among his best-known bridges were the seven-span railroad and highway bridge over the Mississippi at Rock Island, Ill.; the McKinley Bridge at St. Louis, Mo.; the Northern Pacific railroad bridge over the Missouri at Bismarck, N.D.; and bridges over the Columbia and Willamette rivers in Oregon. His double-track railroad bridge over the Ohio River at Metropolis, Ill., contained several striking innovations, including a simple truss span of 720 feet (219 metres) and the unusual use of alloys: silicon steel for the bridge proper and nickel steel for the tension members. He was chief engineer and chairman of the board of engineers of the Benjamin Franklin Bridge over the Delaware River, which, upon completion in 1926, was the longest suspension bridge in the world.

Modjeski was also chief engineer of the Huey P. Long Bridge over the Mississippi at New Orleans and, as his last undertaking, served as chairman of the board of consulting engineers for the San Francisco–Oakland Bay Bridge (California), completed in 1936. By the time he died, on June 26, 1940, in Los Angeles, he had been associated with more than 50 major bridges.

ROBERT MAILLART

Robert Maillart was a Swiss bridge engineer whose radical use of reinforced concrete revolutionized masonry arch bridge design.

Maillart was born on Feb. 6, 1872, in Bern, Switz. After studying at the Swiss Federal Institute of Technology of Zürich, where he received a degree in structural engineering in 1894, Maillart worked for several private engineering firms, collaborating for a time with the French engineer François Hennebique before organizing his own independent practice. In 1901 he built his first bridge, at Zuoz, Switz., over the Inn, an arch whose slenderness and flatness astonished the public and other engineers. Maillart's system was based on an integration of arch, roadway, and stiffening girder into a single monolithic structure, resulting in great aesthetic appeal and large economic savings. For the next 40 years he continued to embellish the Swiss Alps with a variety of graceful arches, of which perhaps the most famous is the curving Schwandbach Bridge, at Schwarzenburg, which has been described as "a work of art in modern engineering."

Maillart also built many other structures, including a number of factories and warehouses in Russia between 1912 and 1919. The Russian Revolution temporarily ruined him financially, but he returned to Switzerland to resume his career. He died on April 5, 1940, in Geneva.

CONCLUSION

The development of railways is one of the great landmarks in the progress of human civilization. Coming early in the 19th century, railways provided an element that was essential to the full realization of the promise of the surging Industrial Revolution—namely, a reliable, low-cost, high-volume system of land transportation. The realization of that promise continues today, in spite of competing transportation systems such as highways and airlines. Along with railways came, inevitably, railway bridges—spans across chasms or over bodies of water that had to be constructed to much higher standards than bridges not intended to bear the weight of heavy freight trains. These structures, too, have a continued use today, as the human race continues to adapt technology to the constant need for moving goods and people across the ever-shrinking face of Earth.

abutment The part of a structure (as an arch or a bridge) that directly receives thrust or pressure.

alternating current An electric current that reverses its direction at regularly recurring intervals.

armature A piece of soft iron or steel that connects the poles of a magnet or of adjacent magnets.

ballast Gravel or broken stone laid in a railroad bed or used in making concrete.

berth A place to sit or sleep especially on a ship or vehicle.

bogie A swiveling railway truck.

caisson A watertight chamber used in construction work under water or as a foundation.

cant n. Inclination; slope. v. To set at an angle.

cantilever To support by a projecting beam or member supported at only one end.

centrifugal Proceeding or acting in a direction away from a centre or axis.

chicanery Deception by artful subterfuge or sophistry.

colliery A coal mine and its connected buildings.

coolie In the 19th century, an unskilled labourer or porter usually in or from the East Asia hired for low or subsistence wages.

couchette A compartment on a European passenger train so arranged that berths can be provided at night.

cruciform Forming or arranged in a cross.

demountable A container designed to allow disassembly with minimum damage to component parts.

diesel A heavy oil used as fuel in diesel engines.

direct current An electric current flowing in one direction only and substantially constant in value.

eyebar A metal bar having a closed loop at one or both ends.

ferromagnetic Of or relating to substances with an abnormally high magnetic permeability, a definite saturation point, and appreciable residual magnetism and hysteresis.

fibre optics The use of thin transparent fibres of glass or plastic that are enclosed by material of a lower refractive index and that transmit light throughout their length by internal reflections.

hinterland A region lying beyond major metropolitan or cultural centres.

hydraulic Operated by the resistance offered or the pressure transmitted when a quantity of liquid (as water or oil) is forced through a comparatively small orifice or through a tube.

maglev The use of magnetic fields generated by superconducting magnets to cause an object (as a vehicle) to float above a solid surface.

megalopolis A thickly populated region centring in a metropolis or embracing several metropolises.

pneumatic Moved or worked by air pressure.

profiteer To make what is considered an unreasonable profit especially on the sale of essential goods during times of emergency.

rectifier A device for converting alternating current into direct current.

regenerative braking Electric braking in which electrical energy that is produced by the motor is transferred to the supply line.

rheostatic Of or relating to a resistor for regulating a current by means of variable resistances.

robber baron An American capitalist of the latter part of the 19th century who became wealthy through exploitation (as of natural resources, governmental influence, or low wage scales).

semaphore An apparatus for visual signaling (as by the position of one or more movable arms).

tamp To drive in or down by a succession of light or medium blows.

telemetry Highly automated communications process by which measurements are made and other data collected at remote or inaccessible points and transmitted to receiving equipment for monitoring, display, and recording.

tensile Of, relating to, or involving tension.

thyristor Any of several semiconductor devices that act as switches, rectifiers, or voltage regulators.

torque A force that produces or tends to produce rotation or torsion.

transformer A device employing the principle of mutual induction to convert variations of current in a primary circuit into variations of voltage and current in a secondary circuit.

BIBLIOGRAPHY

RAILROADS

Current developments in railway transportation are documented and interpreted in *Jane's World Railways* (annual). The history of railway technology is presented in Geoffrey Freeman Allen, *Railways: Past, Present & Future* (1982); George H. Drury (comp.), *The Historical Guide to North American Railroads*, 2nd ed. (2000); Lucius Beebe and Charles Clegg, *Hear the Train Blow: A Pictorial Epic of America in the Railroad Age* (1952); Geoffrey Freeman Allen, *Railways of the Twentieth Century* (1983); and Gustav Reder, *The World of Steam Locomotives* (1974; originally published in German, 1974).

Geoffrey Freeman Allen, *The World's Fastest Trains: From the Age of Steam to the TGV*, 2nd ed. (1992), is a history of high-speed rail through the 20th century by a well-known British railroad writer. Jacob Meunier, *On the Fast Track: French Railway Modernization and the Origins of the TGV, 1944–1983* (2002), explores the technological context and the political decisions that led to the French high-speed system. Christopher P. Hood, *Shinkansen: From Bullet Train to Symbol of Modern Japan* (2006), is a study of the importance of the Shinkansen in modern Japanese identity. Jonathan S. Fischer (ed.), *High Speed Rail: Background and Issues* (2010), is a collection of essays and public documents on issues facing the development of high-speed rail in the United States.

Fred W. Frailey, *Twilight of the Great Trains*, expanded ed. (2010), examines the social and technological forces that brought about the decline of American passenger rail after World War II. Other scholarly, detailed and well-illustrated histories, by a former curator at the Smithsonian Institution, are John H. White, *The American Railroad Passenger Car* (1978); and *The American Railroad Freight Car: From the Wood-Car Era to the Coming of Steel* (1993). Mike Schafer and Mike McBride, *Freight Train Cars* (1999), is a well-illustrated popular history of all types of American freight cars.

Histories of railroads frequently address their social and political impact, as in Nicholas Faith, *The World the Railways Made* (1990); Patrick O'Brien, *Railways and the Economic Development of Western Europe, 1830–1914* (1983); Albro Martin, *Railroads Triumphant: The Growth, Rejection, and Rebirth of a Vital American Force* (1992); and Clarence B. Davis et al. (eds.), *Railway Imperialism* (1991).

Modern traction systems are the subject of Vilas D. Nene, *Advanced Propulsion Systems for Urban Rail Vehicles* (1985); and H.I. Andrews, *Railway Traction: The Principles of Mechanical and Electrical Railway Traction* (1986).

BRIDGES

David P. Billington, *The Tower and the Bridge: The New Art of Structural Engineering* (1983), traces the history of structures since the Industrial Revolution and emphasizes a series of individual engineers who were structural artists. David J. Brown, *Bridges* (1993), chronicles bridge building from its beginnings to projected structures, with discussions of the world's most important bridges, some of which were failures. Eric DeLony (ed.), *Landmark American Bridges* (1993), contains elegantly illustrated presentations of large and small bridges built in the United States from the late 18th century to the post-World War II era, with a time line encapsulating the history of bridges from 1570 to the present.

C.M. Woodward, *A History of the St. Louis Bridge* (1881), on the Eads Bridge, is still the most complete work ever published on one bridge, a classic work for both the non-technical reader and the engineer. David McCullough, *The Great Bridge* (1972, reissued 1982), narrates the political and human history of the building of the Brooklyn Bridge. David P. Billington, *Robert Maillart's Bridges* (1979), gives substantial details of the major works of this bridge designer and builder.

Fritz Leonhardt, *Bridges: Aesthetics and Design* (1984), provides a substantial general discussion and includes a wide selection of striking photographs of old and new bridges. A finely illustrated nontechnical text by Hans Wittfoht, *Building Bridges* (1984), centers on both the design and the construction of bridges. M.S. Troitsky, *Planning and Design of Bridges* (1994), focuses on the selection of bridge type and preliminary design. Walter Podolny, Jr., and John B. Scalzi, *Construction and Design of Cable-Stayed Bridges*, 2nd ed. (1986), treats the modern bridge form and provides substantial technical detail, although the nontechnical reader will understand much of the text. Christian Menn, *Prestressed Concrete Bridges*, trans. and ed. by Paul Gauvreau (1990; originally published in German, 1986), a technical work primarily for engineers, provides historical coverage and deals elegantly with the many complex issues in bridge design. Louis G. Silano (ed.), *Bridge Inspection and Rehabilitation* (1993), is a compendium of practical information.

INDEX